Everyday Miracles is a miracle itself. As an intensive care nurse, Julie Hedenborg had lost all faith in God until a clinically dead patient she resuscitated convinced her he saw all she did while he was "dead." Step by step, God miraculously led Julie back to faith and directed her to share His miracle stories with millions. If you need evidence of God's miracle-working reality or a boost to your faith, this book is a must-read!

John Burke
Founding Pastor Gateway Church
Author of *Imagine Heaven* and *Imagine the God of Heaven*

It is with great enthusiasm that I sincerely endorse this wonderful work from Julie Hedenborg. It is one thing to catalog and publish a book on NDE experiences but Julie does so much more than that. Her own journey to faith and belief in itself is compelling and beautiful. Add to this her ability to articulate the effects on those of us who have taken this unexpected and miraculous journey and you have an inspirational message. Her scriptural references are perfectly matched and her conclusions profound. This is a must-read for those of us who do believe and a tremendous help and encouragement to those who want to believe.

Jim Woodford
Author of *Heaven An Unexpected Journey*

God is doing chest compressions in souls through Julie. He is using her faithful obedience to bring new life to hearts around the globe.

Sheila Preston Fitzgerald
Speaker and Author of *One Foot In Heaven*

I have seen firsthand the amazing ways God can transform somebody's life when they listen to a miraculous testimony shared through a podcast. Julie Hedenborg has carefully selected the absolute best stories from her *Everyday Miracles Podcast* and shared them in this book. As you encounter story after story of God showing up and moving in some of the most unlikely and hopeless circumstances, your faith will be uplifted and you'll begin to have a renewed confidence that God can and will show up in your life for challenges both large and small.

Shaun Tabatt
Publishing Executive, Destiny Image Publishers
Co-author of *Near-Death Experiences, Stories of Heaven and the Afterlife*, and *Real Near-Death Experience Stories*

What an honor and a privilege it is for me to count Julie as a dear sister in the Lord! How I enjoy sharing each episode with the various people in my client base! Through her work Julie brings everyday people into the hope of *Everyday Miracles* from a wonder-working God! Her podcast themes touch and meet the needs of many hearts searching for the reality of a God who interfaces with us in real time. Julie's skilled and gentle guidance elicits powerful keys from her guests that serve to effectively break down walls of fear, "equipping the saints" to embrace a BOLD, CONFIDENT FAITH in a LIVING, PRESENT JESUS!!!

Shelley M Ed.
LFS Ministries

This book has an incredible assortment of miracle testimonies that will ignite your faith for your own breakthrough. It is indispensable for anyone who needs healing or wants to increase their faith for the supernatural.

Steve Austin
Pastor, Author, President of Living Hope Chaplaincy

Riveting, compelling, didn't want to put it down! Julie is so transparent in describing her journey, emotions, and even her own questioning of God Almighty. That is a bold admission! She shared her own personal miracle, and she also brings to life testimonies of individuals who have encountered divine intervention in their own lives. Reading about these miracles and the profound impact they have had on people's lives will no doubt compel YOU to seek the love, goodness, and power of Jesus personally. Julie shares the importance of a personal relationship with Jesus and highlights the profound revelation of His love and grace in her life.

Mary Starr
Speaker and Podcast Host
Awake To Truth Ministry

Julie's heart for others is a bridge to Jesus. This is the gift He has given her to show others the way. He has led her to share a collection of testimonies of various individuals rising from the depths of despair to deliverance. These real-life accounts will resonate with your soul, inspire and heal. Testimonies of God's miraculous power, when least expected, and needed most, will leave you captivated with His love.

Nathan Porter
Clinical Social Work/Therapist, LCSW

Julie is an inspiring example of what God can do through a willing vessel. As a regular listener of the *Everyday Miracles Podcast*, I am thrilled to have this book to read and share with others! The NDE stories have made a profound impact on me, as God has used them to completely release me from a fear of death! As I hear each testimony, I am often reminded of Jesus' words of comfort to Martha, "'I am the resurrection and the life. Anyone who believes in me will live, even after dying. Everyone who lives in me and believes in me will never die...'" (John 11:25-26, NLT). Julie consistently keeps us rooted in Scripture in the midst of these spectacular testimonies. Also vitally important to me is the compelling evidence of the changed lives in these stories, bringing much glory to God.

Marnie Clark
Meet Me in Isaiah Podcast Creator and Host

Everyday Miracles inspired by the Christian podcast of the same name, shares compelling near-death experiences and highlights testimonies that reveal God's miraculous power. Podcasts have become a powerful tool for sharing encouraging messages and spreading the gospel to a global audience. The harvest is ripe, but the laborers a few. Julie is living proof that God can do amazing work with a simple obedience yes.

For those seeking inspiration, encouragement, or a renewed sense of wonder, *Everyday Miracles* is a must-read. It invites readers to join in the journey of discovering God's miraculous presence in the ordinary moments of life, reinforcing the timeless truth that God is actively at work in our world today.

Misty Phillip
Founder of Spark Media

In my 30 years as a clinical neuropsychologist, I have had the honor of walking people through their hardest, most painful journeys to healing and wholeness. Shame often convinces people that their past was broken beyond repair, leaving them feeling unworthy of God's love, grace, mercy, or forgiveness. Yet, once they shared their story, and they brought their secrets out of the darkness into the light of truth, they see how God brings beauty for ashes, and beautiful sacred scars for their painful wounds.

Our personal stories of God's goodness and faithfulness encourages others just a few steps down on the ladder of life. *Everyday Miracles* is a beautiful book highlighting the power of God to change our lives instantaneously or over time, and the importance of sharing such stories to hearten others still waiting for God's answer to their prayers. This book is an inspiring reminder that God still performs miracles, signs, and wonders today!

Dr. Michelle Bengtson
Board-Certified Clinical Neuropsychologist

From the very beginning, *Everyday Miracles* had me on the edge of my seat! I don't think I've ever read a book (other than the Bible) that moved me closer to Jesus. It's been AWESOME to watch the Lord work in Julie's life the last ten years. I watched her go through her difficult health issues, while being an AMAZING wife and mother, to a messenger for Christ through her podcast and writings. You owe it to yourself and your eternal life to read this PHENOMENAL book!

Thomas Elrod
CEO of Compassion Impact Program

Everyday Miracles: Real Firsthand Testimonies that Reveal God's Miraculous Power is a profoundly inspiring and uplifting read that rekindles faith and hope in the modern world. Each account is a testament to the power of faith and the presence of God in our daily lives, offering a refreshing reminder that miracles are not just a thing of the past but a present-day reality. *Everyday Miracles* is more than just a book; it is a beacon of hope and spiritual encouragement.

Sue Detweiler
Author of *Healing Rain*, International Speaker, and Founder of Life Bridge Global

Julie's own inspiring testimony, along with the miraculous stories she shares in her powerful book and podcast, demonstrates how God can use shattering crises to revolutionize our faith and propel us into purpose. When we're reduced to nothing, stripped of hope, Jesus swoops into the void to work wonders. By Christ's power, miracles happen, transforming countless lives when shared. There's a condition for such revolutionary results: If-and that's a big "if"—we surrender ourselves wholeheartedly to Him, as Julie and her subjects did, stumbling uncertainly toward their God-given missions. These riveting accounts highlight that God doesn't call the qualified, He qualifies the called. Apart from Him, indeed, we can do nothing of any lasting value. With Him, all things are indeed possible.

Isabella Campolattro
Author & Speaker

One of these testimonies spoke to me during a personal health crisis. Through prayer and reliance on Christ, I was led into a chain of miraculous events that started with an everyday miracle Julie shared, and ended with me experiencing a full physical healing! God's fingerprints are evident throughout these stories and have awakened me to how much more present He is in my life—today. The personal stories Julie selected are infused with the light of Jesus and are breathing new life into thousands of grateful recipients around the world.

Dave Hooke
Founder of Project Lamplight

Foreword by
JOAN HUNTER

E V E R Y D A Y

32 Real Firsthand Testimonies That Reveal God's Miraculous Power

MIRACLES

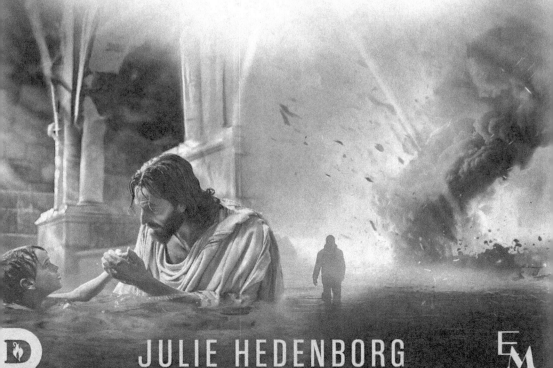

JULIE HEDENBORG

EVERYDAY MIRACLES

32 REAL FIRSTHAND TESTIMONIES THAT REVEAL GOD'S MIRACULOUS POWER

JULIE HEDENBORG

DESTINY IMAGE

Destiny Image P.O. Box 310, Shippensburg, PA 17257-0310

This book and all other Destiny Image's books are available at Christian bookstores and distributors worldwide.

For Worldwide Distribution, Printed in the U.S.A.

Reach us on the Internet: www.destinyimage.com.

ISBN 13 TP: 979-8-8815-0180-8

ISBN 13 eBook: 979-8-8815-0181-5

Dedication

This book is lovingly dedicated to Jesus, my precious Savior and Healer. Your sacrifice on the cross, Your boundless love, and Your answers to my most desperate prayers have shaped my life immeasurably. Serving You is an honor that I cherish deeply. Beyond the miracles, it is the profound revelation of Your love, Your heart, and Your goodness that transforms lives. I eagerly anticipate the day I meet you face-to-face, yet until then, I find joy in sharing the stories of Your divine intervention in our lives.

ACKNOWLEDGMENTS

First and foremost, to my husband, Lars, whose emotional, financial, and spiritual support has been unwavering. Your belief in the impossible has been a beacon during my darkest times.

Thank you to my parents, Marsha and Kendal, who introduced me to Jesus, and nurtured my faith from a tender age.

To my children, Anders and Kendal, thank you for your patience, prayers, and encouragement as I navigate the challenging balance of being a wife, mother, and podcaster. Your support means the world.

I am profoundly grateful to each guest on my podcast who has shared their intimate and transformative experiences. Your stories have not only inspired me but have also touched the lives of countless others, giving glory to God.

A heartfelt thanks to Constance Bounds, for your mentorship and guidance at the inception of my podcasting journey. Your faith in my vision helped turn it into a reality.

To my cousin, Melanie Clark, thank you for your prayers and support during times of doubt. The fruits of this work are a testament to the power of steadfast faith.

Thank you, Christina Hedenborg, for being my early audience when it felt like no one was listening. Your encouragement helped me persevere through the initial silence.

Thanks to Heather Plutt, for helping me to see that each of us has a ministry and can be used by God in ways we can't imagine.

Thank you to Kelly Palombo, for asking me to post one video to YouTube. God used it to lead me to video (which I didn't want or plan). This allowed for testimonies to be seen and heard by millions in countries around the world.

Thanks to Selina Brassil and my Bible study sisters in Christ for covering me in prayer for years, for protection and discernment, for my family, and for my own spiritual development.

Thank you to John and Kathy Burke, for your work in revealing the commonalities of near-death experiences that tie directly to the scriptures, and for establishing solid interpretive keys as we consider these increasing reports. Your work encouraged me to step out as I felt God leading, to share these testimonies, and to keep a biblical foundation as my constant anchor.

To Lilia Samoilo, thank you for your support and friendship. I love your passion in sharing the realities of Jesus, God the Father, heaven, hell, and angels. Your servant heart combined with your expertise has helped so many receive much-needed spiritual healing. The hours of your time volunteering and supporting those that have suffered trauma of various forms will be rewarded in heaven. You are a blessing!

To so many who have supported me and have made it possible to do this work: my amazing PT Dr. Jenn Hause, Brent Doolittle and Candle Rusch for technical expertise, and Nena Wetjen for help at home. Each of you are beautiful blessings in my life!

Lastly, to Destiny Image, for your expertise and passion in making this book what it is meant to be. Your support has been invaluable.

CONTENTS

GOD'S MOSAIC

"This time, people who are just regular people are going to do something that they may think is small and insignificant, and they may not even understand it, but they feel compelled that they're supposed to do this one thing. They'll argue in their own head and say 'That doesn't make any sense. Why would I do that? That's not going to change anything.' And if everybody who hears what they're supposed to do and does just that—nothing more, nothing less—just that, and remains faithful, the lights will come on and you'll see a mosaic that God is working, and everyone on Earth will know that only the God of Abraham, Isaac, and Jacob could have done it."

- Billy Graham

FOREWORD

Supernatural events should be considered normal and natural for every blood-bought, born-again, Spirit-filled believer in Jesus Christ. Every day a Christian is confronted with numerous opportunities to bring peace in conflict, minister healing to the sick, counsel the confused and the hurting and share the truth of the gospel with the lost. The main difference between those who experience miracles by the supernatural power of the Holy Spirit and those who do not, is whether or not they actually believe what the scriptures teach and act on it, while the rest languish in unbelief.

We who profess to know Jesus Christ as our Lord and Savior, have access to the wisdom of Christ and to use the authority of His name to do great works just as He did when He walked the earth in the flesh. It just requires that we surrender to His will, obey His voice and act in faith. A humble heart in submission to the Lord God Almighty has the potential to do all that Jesus did-and we will!

Our responsibility is to obey, because it is He who does the miraculous deeds. As we adopt a lifestyle of obedience and faith, the Holy Spirit has the freedom to use our words to accomplish what only God can do. That sense of helplessness we feel when we are confronted with people in great need, leaves us as we realize the burden for miracles lies totally on His shoulders.

As we learn to depend on God and obey His voice, miracles and supernatural events become normal in our lives. Our faith rises as we observe His responses to our obedience until one day we realize that God can actually do anything through a person who trusts Him. In this way we grow in faith and become naturally supernatural and divine change agents wherever we go. Every believer should fervently desire to be that kind of Christian and you can!!

Blessings Beyond Measure,

Joan Hunter
Author/Evangelist
Host of *Miracles Happen!* TV show

THE MIRACLE THAT SPARKED A JOURNEY

EARLY DAYS OF AN UNLIKELY EVANGELIST

Born in beautiful horse country, the city of Lexington, Kentucky, I was cradled in a community of warmth despite my parents' financial struggles. Loved and cared for, I grew up sensitive, quiet, and respectful of authority. The early divorce of my parents marked a turning point, as I witnessed my mother's relentless efforts to make ends meet. This instilled in me a determination to achieve independence through education and a steadfast career.

My journey to nursing was anything but direct. Eventually, I found my calling in cardiovascular intensive care—a role that resonated deeply with my spirit. After two years in intensive care, I was accepted into graduate school for a Master of Science in nurse anesthesia. Finally, after many years of education and training, I had arrived at what I felt was my calling. It suited me perfectly. I remember praying on the way to see my patients and feeling I was exactly where I was meant to be…until it wasn't.

A FRACTURED FAITH

My journey with the Christian faith, deeply rooted in my upbringing, faced its most significant challenge during my college years. Enrolled and engaged in my studies, I encountered a perspective that starkly contrasted with everything I had known. My favorite professor in Medical Anthropology, Dr. Shannon, whom I admired for his wisdom and charismatic personality, revealed his atheistic beliefs in our conversation before class one day. It would haunt me for years. I will never forget his comment, "Man cannot face their mortality. Religion is their coping mechanism, their modern-day Santa Claus." My heart broke. Suddenly, for the first time, I began to question God and the Bible (approximately 1990).

This statement shook my previously unshakable faith. What if he is right? As personal and various traumas unfolded, these doubts festered, leading me away from the church and into a spiritual wilderness. Many of my choices and actions in these years are not ones I wish to write in this book, but they are part of my testimony. It wasn't until an experience years later that my dying faith would be resuscitated.

HOW ONE MAN'S OUT-OF-BODY EXPERIENCE CHANGED MY LIFE

"I Was Floating Near the Ceiling"
The catalyst for my renewed faith emerged unexpectedly during a routine night shift in 1996-1997 in the cardiovascular intensive care unit. I was tending to an open-heart surgery patient who was slow to awaken from anesthesia, requiring frequent neurological checks. Amidst the quiet of the ICU, a critical alarm sounded. It was from the room of another patient, Mr. Jones, whose heart monitor signaled a life-threatening condition known as ventricular tachycardia. Rushing to his aid, I initiated emergency procedures. Despite our efforts, Mr. Jones was clinically dead; his vital signs flatlined, and his skin turned pale blue.

Just as hope seemed to fade, Mr. Jones miraculously regained consciousness after being unconscious for five to 7 minutes. Suddenly, I heard, "It's about time you came in here." When I looked at his face, I saw that he had regained consciousness! Overjoyed, I played along with him, exclaiming, "Mr. Jones, what are you doing to us?" Once he was stabilized, the staff returned to their other patients. His primary nurse was at the desk charting the code, and I was left alone with him. As I was crouched down to clean the room of stray caps, medication vials, and rhythm strips, he shared something profound.

"Hey, I just want to say thank you," he said, looking down at me. I replied and smiled, "You are so welcome, but that is kind of what they pay me for." He continued looking down at me from his bed as I picked up the debris, and with a more serious tone, "No, I don't think you understand… I saw you." I stopped and looked up at him. He pointed up toward the ceiling, over the foot of his bed, "I was floating right there, near the ceiling and I saw everything that happened. You came into the room after you called for help, and you put the paddles on my chest, and you shocked me. A tall, thin guy in a white lab coat walked in and grabbed this bag that helped me breathe," and he went on to precisely describe every detail of what transpired, everything that was said, who rotated in and out of chest compressions, who called the doctor outside of the room. The phone call outside his room was information he could not have known from his bed, as he was unresponsive and without a pulse.

This testimony was a profound moment for me. The vivid description of his out-of-body experience provided me with undeniable evidence of a conscious existence beyond the physical body. My first thought was that we truly are spirit beings. We are spirits living in a physical body. My kind, brilliant professor was wrong. A tsunami of thoughts came, and tears were emerging. We are spirits. We go somewhere when we leave our bodies. Heaven and hell may be real. The spirit realm is real, so God is real. Could it be? I had the painful realization that I had rejected the very real Jesus, the one who came and died so that I could be forgiven, and my spirit could leave at death and be united with Him.

My heart broke and I felt an overwhelming sense of regret, sorrow, and shame that I had turned away from Jesus for years. My long hair was hiding the tears as I was still crouching. I pleaded in heartache and in my thoughts, "Oh dear Jesus, I am so, so, sorry. I am so sorry." For a moment the shame and regret I felt was almost unbearable. Although I didn't see anything, there was no audible voice, I felt suddenly as if Jesus was standing right there looking down at me on the floor and letting me know, "I love you. I am here and I have always been here." I felt no condemnation. I felt such gratitude for this revelation. It changed my life.

This encounter did more than just resuscitate Mr. Jones; it revived my faith. My cousin Melanie, who was particularly moved by this event, has since shared it with many others. She told me, "Julie, when I tell people about what you witnessed, it really impacts them. Some have even come to faith in Jesus." Looking back, I believe God allowed me to have this experience for several reasons. He was drawing me back to Him, to the truth, through His mercy, grace, and love. The prayers of many might have also contributed to this blessing.

During my two years in intensive care, I heard various accounts from patients who had near-death experiences. Almost all reported seeing a light; many mentioned a tunnel, and some felt a presence they couldn't identify. One person returned from complete darkness terrified, and some even saw deceased relatives.

Some nurse colleagues also shared similar experiences they had witnessed. A few were uncomfortable and would quickly joke to shift the conversation. I'm not sure why my patients felt comfortable sharing their experiences with me, but I believe God used this experience to prepare me for a future calling to draw others to Him. There was so much more to learn, but this event marked a valuable turning point in my life.

GOD SPEAKS

Nearly ten years later, it was a perfect morning in the operating room. I loved everything about being a nurse anesthetist. Like clockwork, our team started the first case of the day with compassion, efficiency, and competence. I clearly remember my healthy patient, a smooth induction of anesthesia, and an easy placement of the breathing tube. Everyone in the room was working in perfect harmony. I was in a wonderful flow state.

As I pivoted to put away my laryngoscope, I can still visualize the scene and hear the words so clearly that were dropped into my thoughts, almost audible, "This part of your life is over." It was such a clear statement in my mind, stated with a calm, matter-of-fact authority. My heart sank. I immediately felt sad and confused. I kept wondering why I would have that thought. It stayed with me. Later that night I would share with my husband. Confused, I kept asking him, "Why would I think that? Why? I just don't understand."

I truly had no idea that God was speaking to me. The perfect Jesus follower would finish her cases for the day, proceed to her manager with complete clarity and obedience, and turn in a resignation. Instead, I was confused and questioning the foods I had eaten within the last day. What toxin had affected my brain?

The clarity and finality of the message left me wrestling with a mix of confusion and profound sadness. Although our family goal included my gradual stepping away from work, the thought of completely departing from a career that I loved and which defined so much of my life was daunting. Yet, the voice spoke with an undeniable certainty, prompting a deep examination of what my future was meant to hold. Within months, I would suffer a traumatic injury to my neck, and my world, my identity was going to change.

THE NECK INJURY: A PIVOTAL MOMENT

I was diagnosed with moderate scoliosis in middle school. Scoliosis, or curvature of the spine, is fairly common, but my case is somewhat unusual. The severity of scoliosis is usually assessed by an X-ray, measuring what's called a Cobb angle, which can vary depending on who's measuring it. In my case, the curvature has been measured at 40 to 66 degrees, which is classified as severe. If you could see my spine from behind, it would look like my first lumbar vertebra in the mid-back has been twisted nearly 90 degrees counterclockwise. This twist causes a noticeable "C" curve in my back, makes my posterior left rib cage stick out, and raises my right hip higher than the left. When I stand relaxed, my belly button is visibly two inches off-center, and I've lost nearly 3 inches in height. I've dealt with chronic pain for as long as I can remember. Fortunately, surgery wasn't considered necessary when I was younger, as my curvature was only in the mid-twenties. However, it worsened significantly in my thirties.

When I was 35, my then-boyfriend encouraged me to see his chiropractor, who was shocked by my x-ray. He considered my case rare and was hesitant to perform traditional adjustments, opting instead to use a Pro-adjuster which clicked as it moved over my back. He advised against any activities that involved twisting or bending, such as vacuuming, using a dishwasher, doing laundry, golfing, bowling, biking, and dancing. He also warned that my condition could reduce my lifespan by 15 years and affect my ability to have children, which devastated me. I even offered my boyfriend, Lars, the chance to leave, knowing he wanted children, but he stayed, married me, and has been a constant support.

Several months after the divine directive, "This part of your life is over," echoed in the operating room, I faced a significant and unexpected challenge that would redirect the trajectory of my life.

AN ADJUSTMENT IN EVERY SENSE OF THE WORD

At 45, I experienced what I can only describe as a dramatic shift. This change was precipitated by what seemed at first a minor decision—a routine adjustment during a chiropractic visit. This was the fourth chiropractor I had consulted in hopes of relief for my chronic pain.

On that particular day, I reported a persistent kink in my neck to my chiropractor, a symptom that was unusual for me but felt particularly bothersome. I had always exercised caution when it came to neck manipulations, largely due to the warnings I'd heard from neurology colleagues about the risks associated with such procedures. However, trusting in the expertise of my chiropractor, I consented to an adjustment.

The chiropractor assessed my condition and identified that the second cervical vertebra (C2) was misaligned. I knew there were risks and I agreed to the adjustment, hoping it would provide relief. The chiropractor performed the manipulation, which involved quick and vigorous twists to my neck. I heard three levels of my neck make a cracking sound on the first twist, which was followed by an immediate sense of release. Initially, the adjustment seemed to have resolved the discomfort, yet I felt very lightheaded and dizzy.

However, the relief was short-lived. As I walked out of the chiropractor's office, I began to experience a new pain in my neck. Headaches followed and worsened over days. The range of motion in my neck decreased. By the end of the week I was unable to turn my head. The neck pain became constant and intense, unresponsive to any over-the-counter pain medications, and it was accompanied by dizziness. The pain would wake me up at night.

Concerned by these developments, I contacted my chiropractor again, explaining the severity of my symptoms and seeking further advice. His office had no availability for appointments. I chose to wait.

Nine days after my neck adjustment, a disturbing incident occurred while discussing my child's progress with his tutor in the kitchen. Suddenly, my vision blurred and I saw stars; the left side of her face appeared distorted, and although I could see her mouth moving on the right side, I couldn't hear a word she said. I wasn't sure if it was the visual distortion that distracted me from what she was saying, or if there was an actual loss of hearing. This episode was brief but left me completely disoriented and embarrassed. I apologized to the tutor, explaining that something strange had happened with my vision and hearing. On her way out, she looked at me with concern, asking if I was okay, to which I uncertainly suggested it might be due to a low blood sugar.

As the children were eager to have some summer fun, I decided we should go to the pool. I was in the kitchen grabbing a pool bag when an intense and indescribable urgency overwhelmed me. A feeling of urgency flooded over me from my head to my toes that left a ripple effect of goosebumps over my entire body. The message was alarming. The unmistakable message was clear: go to the emergency room (ER) *right now!*

My mother-in-law arrived at this moment to find me standing in complete shock at what I had just experienced. I was confused, unaware of the severity of my injury. I was also annoyed because the last place a nurse wants to go is to an ER. The wait times, the exposure to exotic germs, and the expense are considerable. Even so, the message compelled me to go. My mother-in-law took over caring for the children as I made the unwise decision to drive myself to the ER. (If you experience vision changes, please do NOT drive a car.) Fortunately, I arrived safely.

At the ER, the initial examination and bloodwork showed nothing abnormal, but I insisted something was seriously wrong due to my vision changes. Reluctantly, the doctor ordered a CT scan with contrast to rule out any unseen issues. The results were shocking: both of my vertebral arteries had dissected, and I had a pseudoaneurysm. One of the dissections was particularly "impressive," and the doctor was astonished that I was still conscious and coherent, suggesting the vision changes were likely due to strokes.

While I believe the neck treatment I received contributed to these critical conditions, it is important to note that there is no definitive proof that this was the cause. Amidst this crisis, friends were texting about what to bring for a party I had planned the next day, oblivious to the seriousness of my situation. An ambulance and a neurosurgeon were being arranged for my transfer to a specialized unit downtown as I was receiving texts about brownies and lemonade. My husband was on a flight home and unaware. I was a patient in critical condition at the same hospital where I am normally one rushing to help in times of emergency. Everything felt very surreal.

Alone momentarily, tears started to fall, and when my compassionate nurse checked on me, I absurdly asked if my July 4th party was officially canceled, trying to find a sliver of normalcy in a surreal situation. We shared a brief laugh—a welcome respite from the tension.

As I was prepared for transfer, I pondered the overwhelming sense of urgency that had gripped me earlier—was it a neurological symptom related to lack of blood flow or something supernatural? This question lingered until, weeks later, a clear answer would come in a most unexpected way, affirming the profound and possibly divine nature of that compelling urge to seek help.

MY AMBULANCE PRAYER

Lying in the back of an ambulance, I overheard the paramedic speaking with the driver and realized my situation was critical. Two arteries to my brain were dissected, one of them badly, (bilateral vertebral artery dissections) and I had a pseudoaneurysm. Side note: you never want to hear "impressive" in your CT or MRI report. It is the one time the goal is to be "unremarkable." I overheard the EMT speaking to the driver and emphatically stating, "This needs to be a smooth ride…not a pothole, not a speed bump. We will need to take a special route." The tone was serious.

As I googled a prognosis, the first thing to surface, "For those that survive…" the painful realization flooded over me that I may not be going home. Blood clots typically form within the dissected arteries and can be dislodged and travel directly to the brain, causing a massive stroke and death. Nobody could reassure me that I was going to be OK. Forty-five years old with two young children and a husband who I may not see again.

Thoughts were swirling in my mind. Did I live out the plans that God had for my life? Did my family know just how much I love them? My heart was racing, my throat tightening and eyes welling up with tears. All I could do was close my eyes and pray, **"God, I am not ready to leave my family. I don't want to go yet. "Lord, please let me share you with just one more person."** I had no idea how God was going to answer that ambulance prayer of July 3, 2015.

By the grace of God, I left the neuro-intensive care unit after three days without any serious life-altering deficits. My injuries were managed medically. Although they said for the next 90 days I could have another stroke, and "the aneurysm probably wouldn't rupture."

The following year and the choices made would prove to be pivotal in my life and faith walk. After a few weeks of driving restrictions, I returned briefly to my job as a nurse anesthetist before severe scoliosis rendered me disabled for my job in 2016. In retrospect, God was redirecting me. There was healing and growth that needed to take place before I could see His plan unfold.

CONFIRMATION OF THE SUPERNATURAL

God showed up in so many amazing ways during this time to let me know He was there. One that really blew me away was weeks after the injury. I was still dealing with considerable pain and anxiety. There were still risks for another stroke or for the aneurysm to rupture, but my doctor cleared me to go on a family cruise in Alaska that we had already paid for in full. I had restrictions on my activity, and he gave me my medical records to allow me to travel. I kept asking God what exactly happened in the kitchen that day. Was it something from Him or was it something that was happening in my brain? Afterall, it was a neurological injury.

We enjoyed a tourist excursion on a large fishing boat. As we traveled back to the dock the captain emerged and shared a testimony. He shared about a time he went fishing with a friend out in the middle of remote Alaskan waters. The fish were biting, and the men lost track of the time. It started getting dark, and they realized their boat had a leak and was filling with water. They soon found themselves in darkness and frigid water as their boat rapidly sank. He and his friend were trying to stay alive and afloat in the dark in the remote, icy water.

The boat captain shared with emotion how he was sure he and his friend were going to die. There was a fisherman returning not too far from their location. The captain shared that the fisherman reported, "Suddenly I felt a powerful sensation flood through my body that I have never felt before. It told me to redirect the boat." It was an urgency that flooded through him, and he had goosebumps and felt compelled to turn his boat in a different direction, heading nowhere into the darkness.

Although it felt pointless, the urgency was so strong that he followed this prompting. It led him straight to the young men who were close to freezing from hypothermia and/or drowning in a remote area where no boat typically travels. Their lives were saved because of this prompting! The faith of all the men involved was stirred. They were so grateful to God for the miracle. This captain was so affected that he was still passionately sharing about his amazing God.

What the fisherman experienced was exactly what I experienced that day in the kitchen. This was such confirmation to me that what I experienced was not a symptom of my neurological trauma. It was not a lack of blood flow. It was not some bizarre neurotransmitter response. It was supernatural. It may have saved my life.

The realization that God (or His messengers) actively stepped into my kitchen, that He cared, and that He saved me from possible death, paralysis or a massive stroke was mind-boggling. This certainty was such a comfort during this time when I was battling with so many mixed emotions.

FULL SURRENDER

The year after my injury was one of physical and emotional healing and spiritual transformation. The realization that God spared me from devastation and possible death is difficult to put into words.

There was much to process those first weeks home. I knew God had protected me and spared me. Despite this miracle, I struggled with anxiety, fear, and righteous anger around the circumstances and the way they were handled. God taught me lessons in forgiveness, in trusting Him, in the power of prayer, and the need for community that year. His grace for this period of my life was remarkable.

I had been a Christian most of my life, yet I was terrified to fully surrender my life to Jesus. What if Jesus asked me to sell everything I own and move to Africa and eat bugs? The images in my mind of giving up my comfort for a ministry in a dangerous and poverty-stricken land were not pretty. Drinking water full of the parasites I had studied in my medical anthropology class, and those man-eating snakes? I imagined what my little starving, bug-phobic scoliotic body outline would look like horizontal inside one of those reptiles. "Yep, see this curve? Definitely her." Of course, I would have to do whatever He asked, right? It's Jesus, the one who died for me. No way I was risking it. For years I let Jesus in, but I only invited Him to be Lord of pieces of my life so beyond repair they were only salvageable by God (i.e, my dating life at age 35). I put Jesus in the corner at a safe distance with limited access.

It wasn't until after the injury at age 45 that I realized my life was spared out of His mercy and grace-and that is the ONLY reason I am still here. It hit me that my time here is now purely bonus time that I couldn't have earned. Finally, after being so afraid to surrender truly and completely, I got down on my knees in tears on my bedroom floor and cried out to God. With everything I had, I thanked God for sparing my life,

"Lord, thank You for saving me and giving me my health. I am completely and forever Yours. I will do whatever You want me to do, anything. I love You." This cry was not driven from a place of obligation for the bonus time He had granted, it was heartfelt and sincere. I meant it with every cell in my body. I was wrecked with gratitude, humility, and a hunger for more of Him.

> "You will find me when you seek me with ALL of your
> heart. "
> - *Jeremiah 29:13 (NIV)*

For some, this type of surrender is followed by a supernatural encounter. I did not experience this, and I would imagine that a supernatural encounter is generally the very rare exception, but I cannot say for sure. I can say as I continued to pursue Him in the Bible and through study with my Bible study group, things began to happen. I began to learn how to hear His voice. At times I would feel His presence. At times I would seek and seek Him, and I couldn't hear anything at all. My blossoming relationship with Jesus at this time I can only describe as patient, loving and gentle.

During the year after my injury, I was also learning some valuable lessons around forgiveness, trusting God, and being obedient. I knew God was doing something. At times I was eager for Him to just show me and wondered if I missed my calling. "I trust you God. I know you have a plan. Help me in this time between. Remove whatever is blocking me from You. Equip me for whatever is coming next."

Reflecting on my full surrender, the most pivotal part of the early journey, I can now clearly see its effects in my life. It was the lighter fluid on my little resuscitated spark of faith. The Bible came alive to me for the first time. I began to feel His promptings more frequently, to feel His gentle and loving conviction, and His heart in a new way. Who knew His plan would be better than my own? Why did I wait so long?

GOD'S CALL TO SHARE TESTIMONIES: A VISION FROM GOD

While attending a business-coaching conference in California with my husband Lars and several guests, I believed I was just there to support him. During a session by Brendon Burchard, who discussed various business promotion strategies, the word *podcast* on the screen caught my attention as if spotlighted. In that instant, I felt a profound clarity and certainty that I was meant to launch a podcast—a library of testimonies.

I was so excited to share this epiphany with my husband, who was somewhere in the room doing a breakout with a small group. As I turned, so thrilled to find him and share, my eyes vigorously scanned the room. Suddenly, I saw a striking and dynamic image that unfolded before my eyes on the large back wall of the conference area. It began at the floor level, as if an invisible hand wielded a large pencil or chalk, sketching side to side and upward. Before me appeared a series of rectangular slabs, resembling stones or tablets, each one representing a unique testimony or story. These slabs were drawn one after another in a swift, back-and-forth motion, creating an effect of continuous construction.

As each new slab appeared, the ones at the bottom of the stack started to fade, giving the impression of an ever-evolving monument. This stack grew taller and taller, extending far above and into the clouds. I could not see the top beyond the encircling clouds. The remaining slabs lit up brightly from the bottom to the top, then faded.

This illumination suggested a divine presence, blessing the testimonies and giving them a sacred significance. The monument's purpose was to bring glory to God while inspiring hope and faith for all types of people.

The clarity and certainty of the vision were overwhelming for me. I felt a deep connection to the purpose revealed to me—a call to gather and share these testimonies through a podcast, providing a platform for voices that inspire and uplift, forming a lasting monument to faith and hope in the world.

I've never been more certain of anything. Excited and expectant, I couldn't stop sharing my thoughts about the potential of this podcast with my husband, believing strongly in what God intended to accomplish through it.

THE RUBBER MEETS THE ROAD

After all the excitement, I almost chickened out. It was 2018 and podcasts were just becoming popular. The only thing I had to qualify me for this calling was a heart to give God glory and a willingness to do whatever He said. I was just learning how to hear His voice, just beginning to really study the Bible. I didn't listen to podcasts. I didn't know anything about interviewing people, or the technical pieces of setting up a platform. I had written in medical shorthand with abbreviations and symbols for over 20 years and now I am to write the notes for episodes. Was God sure? Isn't there someone else more suited?

I did what every terrified person does when they don't want to be obedient. I asked God to send me a sign. It sounds better when we call it, "seeking clarity," but let's be honest, I was scared. I didn't want to look foolish. Most importantly, I didn't want to let God down. I didn't want to commit to something that was going to be hard. Lars was the only person who knew. I hesitated. I got an invite to my Pentecostal friend's small group, and I decided to go and pray with the women, with no plan to share.

I entered Regina's welcoming home to find the women from our prayer group gathered around Samantha, a young woman whose frailty belied the miraculous story of her recent healing. "Samantha has a testimony! She was within hours of death, and God has healed her!" the women exclaimed, their voices filled with praise and awe. Feeling a clear nudge from the Lord, I waited for a quieter moment when Samantha was alone. Approaching her, I tentatively shared my idea in a soft voice, "You know, I'm not sure, but I'm thinking about starting a podcast where people can share their testimonies like yours."

Before I could continue, Samantha stood up in excitement. Her face lit up with joy and tears began to flow. "This is the answer to my prayers! You are the answer to my prayers! YES! I would love to be on your miracle podcast show!" Her enthusiastic response drew the attention of everyone in the room. Regina quickly gathered the group and announced, "God is moving in this room! Julie please share what's happening!" Suddenly, all eyes were on me, and I felt an unmistakable confirmation from God about starting the podcast. It was clear He even had a sense of humor about the dramatic way this was unfolding. I definitely got my sign.

With renewed determination and a sense of divine calling, I prayed fervently, the boldest prayer I knew how to pray at that time, **"God, I have this back issue. I am not sure how long I can do this. I will do this for You if You want me to do it."** Inspired, I began compiling a list of potential testimonies to feature.

Encouraged by a friend, I met with Constance, a Spirit-filled mentor at a local charismatic church. After sharing my aspirations and apprehensions, she looked deeply into my eyes and affirmed, "You are a builder." She anointed my hands with oil, prayed over me, and encouraged me to read Nehemiah, a gesture that filled me with hope and a renewed sense of mission.

My husband Lars was instrumental in bringing the podcast to life. Despite my reservations about using video, he set up a YouTube channel and encouraged me to embrace it. After recording the introductory episode numerous times, his encouragement to just publish it pushed me to finally share it. I only published the audible podcast version and refused his push for video.

This sequence of events, from the divine nudge at Regina's house to the support and encouragement from a few close individuals, underscored the podcast's potential impact. It was not just about sharing testimonies; it was about building a community of faith and witness within my local circle. I posted the first intro with the promise of a list of exciting testimonies and guests. To my dismay, every guest except sweet Samantha said no way. I found myself quickly humbled.

"God, I know you called me to this," I said. The next thing I said was critical, **"Lord, will You show me what YOU want? Will You lead me?"** I heard nothing. I felt discouraged, left it with God, and departed for a hair appointment. I remember my hairdresser rinsing the color from my hair and asking me with a raised voice, "What is this podcast you were telling me about?" I replied, "I am going to share miracles to give God glory."

Immediately, the only other client in the salon, with her head also in the sink, yells out, "I have a miracle testimony!" Evalee did have a miracle testimony. I still have her little scrap piece of paper with her number and healing miracle written in pencil framed in my office. She was the first testimony.

From that moment on, as I sought His direction, God would continue to lead me to people in the craziest of ways. Initially, I had to understand that it wasn't about my plan. It was about surrendering to His plan. I prayed regularly. I met people in airports, grocery stores, at school, on a big rock in Aruba, you name it. My husband even said once, "If I didn't see it myself, I wouldn't believe it." While I now have more guests than I can record, I honestly miss this aspect of seeing God's hand so clearly in the early days, perfectly timed.

As I began to record with guests, I encouraged them to share the low moments as they felt comfortable. I assumed listeners tuned in to hear the big undeniable miracles (and they are spectacular), but interestingly, listeners genuinely connected to the part of the testimony where the guest vulnerably shared the low moments. The platform began to evolve as a safe place for people to feel heard, feel understood, human, but most importantly, it highlighted a lifeline for hope through Jesus.

DIVINE DIRECTION

My vision for the podcast was to share testimonies within the walls of my own church. As I received testimonies from people from different Christian denominations, I prayed for wisdom and discernment. Despite belonging to various denominations, my friends and I share the Christian faith, though we do differ slightly in our practices and ideas. Initially, I was hesitant to share testimonies from outside my church, amusingly assuming that everyone in my church held identical theological beliefs. Even within my own Bible study group, we have varying views on the rapture. Initially, I decided to play it safe and only share testimonies from within my church, thinking it was the safest route.

While not even pondering the podcast, a voice in my head challenged me, "So, miracles only happen to people at your church?" This jolted me and made me laugh as I responded internally, "Of course not, miracles can happen to anyone." Yet, I hesitated, concerned about promoting potentially flawed theology. But the voice persisted, clearly instructing, "Just keep me at the center." This encouraged me to continue, always seeking discernment through prayer.

Early in my podcast journey I received my first testimony of a man who claimed that he had a heavenly experience. Although I had gotten a taste of this in my critical-care experiences, I was not expecting this. It came on the heels of fervent prayer time after I asked God to send me something powerful, unmistakably from Him, that would be used in a powerful way to bring Him glory and make Him known. Initially I was curious, excited, but I wanted to be sure it was from God. I prayed more about this. I searched scripture. I found John Burke's *Imagine Heaven* book on YouVersion about near-death experiences (NDEs) and how many commonalities align with scripture. His work was a big factor in my decision to move forward with these shares.

Even still, I asked God to confirm it. Two women popped into my mind. Both women were in their worn-out Bibles constantly and knew the Word of God. Both women had given me words from the Lord that were true. I had no idea what their thoughts were on NDEs. I prayed over this for days and then I went to each one and asked them what their thoughts were on these reports. The first woman shared that her father had a near-death experience, and this is what initially brought her whole family to faith. I was shocked. I had no idea. They kept his experience within the family.

I went to my other trusted and respected friend and asked for her thoughts. "What is your concern?" she asked. "Well, I want the focus to be on Jesus. I want to be biblically accurate. I don't want the focus to be on the supernatural elements." She replied, "Julie, God *IS* supernatural." I received that as the confirmation I needed.

Ken Johnson, a retired air traffic controller who nearly died of H1N1 flu, was the first heaven testimony I shared. The key beautiful takeaway message: God is real, and He loves us more than we can possibly imagine. Around the time I recorded his testimony I was asked to speak at a Bible study. With his permission, I shared a snippet of Ken's video testimony.

A woman attending asked me if I would share Ken's full video testimony online. I was very reluctant to do this, but I asked Ken, and he was happy for me to share it on YouTube. I posted this for one woman. My videos have now been viewed by millions across the globe (this includes my content on Destiny Image's channel). Ken's testimony was discovered by Guideposts, and they have published it in a book with even further reach. It is funny that as I reached out to get his consent to be shared in this book, he was on a cruise ship and the crew was watching his testimony five years later. God is reaching people through testimonies!

After sharing Ken's testimony, I was flooded with listeners who shared with me their own personal experiences with the afterlife. Many did not have a desire to come and share on my show, they were just so happy to find a safe place to share their experience.

AN IMPORTANT NOTE ABOUT NEAR-DEATH TESTIMONIES

If you are new to your faith, it's crucial to understand the existence of a spiritual realm and the potential danger it poses. Some Christians dismiss all near-death and supernatural testimonies. I agree that there is a need for discernment and caution. Without a solid biblical foundation, exploring these testimonies is like navigating a minefield. Scripture provides guidance on where the dangers lie, as pastor John Burke points out with his "interpretive keys" for understanding these experiences. (see *Imagine the God of Heaven*.)

We must remember that we have an enemy who aims to steal, kill, and destroy us (John 10:10), often masquerading as a "being of light" (2 Corinthians 11:14.) The Bible also warns against engaging with mediums, tarot cards, and new-age practices. All testimonies are subjective, and it's essential to always align them with Scripture, relying on the discernment provided by the Holy Spirit. The Bible should always serve as the basis for our understanding.

So why do I share near-death testimonies? I feel led by God to share these testimonies and I have witnessed them ignite faith and transform lives. From agnostics and atheists to children, sparking a newfound interest and understanding of the Bible. Many return with messages that resonate deeply: **"Tell them what you saw, tell them I am coming soon, tell them they are loved more than they could imagine."** Pastor John Burke suggests these testimonies might be God's way of "coloring in the scriptures" to enhance our understanding of the exciting future that awaits us. These shares have brought the Bible to life for many, encouraging a personal relationship with Jesus.

The feedback from listeners has confirmed the impact of these testimonies. One listener shared how the show rekindled her stalled faith, while another mentioned that a near-death testimony led her to read the entire Bible and develop a deeper relationship with Jesus. My goal is always to direct people toward Jesus and His Word, praying that these testimonies fulfill His purpose.

UNEXPECTED BLESSINGS ALONG THE WAY I HOPE TO SHARE WITH YOU

I began recording powerful testimonies in 2018. Five years into the podcast, the stack of testimonies continues to grow. The irony in the journey? I thought I was going to be used by God to show people that God is very real and present. However, the person who continues to learn the most in this journey might be yours truly. I have been so honored to connect with so many different people who have bravely shared from their hearts some of the most personal and transformative events they have experienced. Their testimonies have inspired me and led me to have a deeper revelation of this very personal and ever-present God. It has changed me and blessed me in more ways than I could have ever expected.

As you read a sample of the testimonies in the following chapters, I pray that you see God's presence in your life and find hope for any challenges you face, whether for healing, provision, or peace. Let these stories connect your heart with His.

Remember, as Philippians 3:8, states, "Yes, everything else is worthless when compared with the infinite value of knowing Christ Jesus my Lord."

CHAPTER 1
A MAN'S 11-HOUR JOURNEY IN HEAVEN

"In him we have redemption through his blood, the forgiveness of sins, in accordance with the riches of God's grace. "
- Ephesians 1:7 (NIV)

His nickname was "Diamond Jim." He enjoyed success, substantial wealth, and a loving family. A traveler at heart, Jim had a passion for flying and business. He was ambivalent when it came to matters of faith. And then he died. An unintentional overdose of medication left him clinically brain-dead for 11 hours. As his family was advised to make funeral arrangements, Jim was experiencing the most unforgettable and transformative journey of his life. I am blessed to see the joy of the Lord in Jim, and the sincerity and compassion he carries for others. I believe he was handpicked by God Himself to share this message! - Julie

My name is **Jim Woodford**. I began my career as a pilot around the time of the Vietnam War, a period when there was a dire shortage of pilots. Many Canadian pilots, including myself, filled positions left vacant as American pilots joined the military. This early part of my life was adventurous, flying from one country to another, eventually visiting 52 countries. I not only flew planes but also ventured into businesses, living a life that many might describe as the American-Canadian dream.

Raised Catholic in Newfoundland and Labrador, spirituality was part of my upbringing, though it didn't deeply resonate with me at the time. I always saw myself as a traveler, exploring the world, unaware that my most profound journey lay ahead—a journey beyond this world to what I once dismissed as mere legend: Heaven.

My testimony isn't just about my experiences but also about overcoming the cynicism and skepticism prevalent in today's world. I understand why people doubt; the world encourages disbelief in anything beyond the tangible. However, despite the insults and skepticism, I am overwhelmed by thousands who find hope and meaning in my experience.

My nickname was "Diamond Jim" because everything I touched turned to gold. I thrived in business and adventure, never suspecting that God's hand was guiding me. I never recognized this divine presence, busy as I was with my earthly pursuits.

However, everything changed in 2014 when I began to feel unwell. My condition deteriorated quickly, despite initial dismissals by medical professionals. It was only when my symptoms worsened that I was diagnosed with Guillain-Barré Syndrome, a rare disorder where the body's immune system attacks the nerves. Weakness and tingling in my extremities soon escalated to a life-threatening emergency.

The moment of my passing was as sudden as it was profound, happening not in the sterile confines of a hospital, but in the solitude of my truck, parked in a remote area as I sought a brief escape from my daily struggles. On that fateful day, overwhelmed by the relentless progression of Guillain-Barré Syndrome and burdened by constant, debilitating pain, I sought solace in the tranquility of the countryside as I set out to check some property markers. As the sun began to set, casting its last warm rays over the landscape, I hoped for a few moments of respite. However, driven to desperation by my suffering, I mistakenly took an excessive dose of my medication, seeking relief that doctors could no longer provide.

The reaction was immediate and terrifying. Instead of the expected easing of my pain, an intense burning sensation surged through my limbs. This pain, unlike any I had felt before, seemed to consume me from within, creating an unbearable sense of panic and disorientation.

As my physical distress intensified, I struggled desperately for air as if drowning, each breath shorter and more labored than the last. Simultaneously I felt an overwhelming feeling of grief and shame. Suddenly, deep within me, I had this feeling that I had this wonderful life, and never once had I thanked or acknowledged the creator. It was at that moment that I knew I was dying. There was an overwhelming sense of loss and purpose. I raised my violently trembling hand and I said the first three of six words that would make all the difference on this journey. "God, forgive me," I cried out toward the setting sun just before my head hit the steering wheel.

As my earthly senses failed, a profound transformation occurred. The pain and grief that had gripped me gave way to an unexpected serenity. The heavy overcoat of pain was completely gone! The sun was beautiful just at the horizon. I heard the birds and smell the grass and I am reveling in the view. I felt amazing, like I was young again.

Looking back momentarily, I notice there is a man sitting in my truck. I was filled with rage. It wasn't until I moved closer that I realized it was me! My own body was slumped over the steering wheel, lifeless and still, a surreal and unsettling sight. Yet, there was no time to linger on this image, as my attention was drawn irresistibly forward. Ahead of me, a brilliant portal of light appeared, unlike anything I had ever seen. It shimmered with a spectrum of colors that defied description, pulsating with energy and emitting a warm, inviting glow.

This portal seemed to stand as a gateway between the earthly realm and something far more profound and expansive. As I moved toward it, drawn by an inexplicable pull, the surroundings of my physical existence faded into the background, replaced by a sense of anticipation and wonder. Crossing the threshold of this portal, I felt an overwhelming rush of peace and clarity—a stark contrast to the chaos and pain of my final moments in the physical world.

Let me tell you about the landscape I encountered—it was like nothing on Earth. Imagine colors so vivid they vibrated with intensity, and scenery so breathtakingly spectacular it seemed painted by divine hands. I walked on grass that literally sparkled beneath my feet, each blade perfect, luminous, casting off a soft light that pulsed as if alive. Above me, the sky boasted a blue so deep it felt like you could dive into it. And the air—it was filled with fragrances and music so heavenly, so beyond our human senses, it just defied any description I could give.

But, as wondrous as this journey was, it took a darker turn. I came across areas where the vibrant green grass shifted to scorched earth, leading to a deep, foreboding chasm. It was a jarring contrast—the beauty and peace of heaven starkly opposed by the isolation that came from being cut off from such divinity.

As I moved closer to understand this, a terrifying encounter unfolded. There, emanating darkness and malice, was a creature that seemed the very embodiment of evil. This moment was one of both profound fear and clarity—the reality of evil was as tangible as the goodness I had just experienced. Chillingly, this being knew me by name, an acknowledgment that shook me deeply, striking fear into my heart. When its eyes locked with mine, I could feel its intense hatred for mankind. It emitted a foul stench of death and decay. I could hear the screams of souls coming from this evil creature. I felt terror when this being called me by my name.

In the midst of that terrifying encounter, when the malevolent presence seemed almost overwhelming, I cried out the last three of the most important six words I could speak. "God, help me!" My salvation came in a truly spectacular fashion. Above me, the sky suddenly brightened—a convergence of lights that seemed to gather strength and purpose as they approached. These lights, brilliant and pure, coalesced into forms of unmistakable power and grace: angels. Their arrival was not just a visual spectacle but a profound reassurance of protection. As they descended, the atmosphere charged with a palpable sense of authority and peace. The angels, radiant and formidable, positioned themselves between me and the darkness, their presence a clear barrier against the malevolence that sought to reach me.

The lead angel, a majestic figure radiating an intense light, stepped forward. With a commanding gesture, he extended his hand toward the looming darkness. From his palm emanated a beam of pure, white light—a weapon of divine origin, targeted directly at the demon. The impact was immediate; the creature recoiled as if struck by a physical force, its form shimmering and breaking apart under the intensity of the light. This light was not just a physical deterrent but a manifestation of divine power, cleansing the area of the dark presence and filling the space with a serene glow. The demon, unable to withstand the purity of the light, vanished into the shadows from whence it came, leaving behind a calm that settled over the area like a comforting blanket.

With the immediate threat dispelled, the angels turned their attention to me. Their expressions were not of triumph but of gentle reassurance. They moved with a grace that belied their formidable power, approaching me with an air of solemnity. The lead angel, whose presence was both awe-inspiring and comforting, spoke softly, his voice resonating with a warmth that seemed to heal and fortify my spirit. **"Fear not,"** he said, a simple phrase that carried with it the weight of profound protection. **"You are safe now; the darkness cannot prevail where there is light."** Their words were powerful, soothing the lingering fear from my encounter, and reinforcing my newfound understanding of the spiritual guardianship afforded to us in our most dire moments.

The angels guided me through a vibrant landscape, this place was alive with lush, radiant flora and a sense of peace that permeated every inch of the environment. As we walked, the gentle touch of their wings and the soothing timbre of their voices healed the deepest fears and wounds within my spirit. This journey through such a miraculous setting began to mend my fractured soul.

I was shown a landscape of the holy city. I was stunned at the size and beauty of the buildings and their warmth. They seemed to be carved of light. The streets were gold, but not the gold of Fort Knox. It is a transparent gold without any impurities. They showed me the halls of learning, the halls of music, and more. I could see people and families that were being reunited. There was one building that stood out to me with a gentler light. In front of it was a huge green space with thousands of children playing with dogs, cats, birds and deer. The guardian explained that this is the nursery of heaven. "This is a home for the souls of children lost on

Earth. Their light is so precious to God and they are cared for here," replied the guardian.

The climax of my spiritual journey occurred when I met Jesus Christ in an indescribably profound encounter. I realized I had not seen one of the guardians in some time. I was in a heavenly paddock-like area near horses when I turned to my side and noticed a profile of a tall figure with one of the guardians kneeling. They were looking at something. There was a shimmer that was over the tall figure's face, almost the appearance of heat rising off of asphalt in the summer. I was intrigued by the glow of the tall figure. It was almost like a liquid golden light was surrounding Him. It was flowing down the slope toward me. When that liquid light hit the flowers they bloomed even more beautifully.

I watched the scene in amazement and sank to my knees. The instant the liquid light encircled me, this feeling of knowledge rose inside me and I realized that the figure I am looking at is no other than the Son of God. Someone I thought was a dusty Jewish legend all my life. Jesus and the guardian had been reading this thin little booklet. It was no bigger than a diner menu. Images of my life came off the pages. I saw things I did in my life. The good and the bad, but worst of all I felt the pain I had caused others. I am eternally sorry for the hurt I caused.

The guardian turned to me and asked, "Jim, what have you done with the life my Master gave you?" I had no answer. Just as the thin book was closed, the knowledge came to me that this was the book of my life. *My* life, that I had considered to be the epitome of success. This was all I had to show for a life? I was filled with so much shame that I wanted to hide. I had so many resources. I could have been more loving, more forgiving, more caring, more generous. The angel disappeared and Jesus turns toward me.

His presence was powerful yet filled with a peace that's hard to describe. I saw the scars on His wrists—vivid marks of His crucifixion, symbolizing the ultimate sacrifice and redemption. His captivating eyes, filled with an infinite love for me and sadness for the world, met mine. He smiled at me with the most beautiful smile. Jesus spoke directly to me. It was both commanding and kind as He instructed me, saying, **"Go back and tell your brothers and sisters of the wonders we have shown you."**

Reluctantly, I was guided back to the physical world by the angels. The journey back was filled with introspection about the implications of my celestial encounters for my personal faith and the message I was now charged to share. Though part of me yearned to stay in that divine presence, I understood my purpose was to return and testify to the spiritual truths I had been shown.

Reflecting on the experience of seeing my book of life, I live each day now to try and be the best man I can be. I strive to be kinder, more forgiving, loving and generous. When I go back to heaven, with God's permission, and I see Jesus open my book of life, I like to think He will need a forklift and five angels to open it. Remember, Jesus has a sense of humor. I have gotten so involved in this little ministry of mine in hopes that people will see how wonderful Jesus is and how we can help one another. I am truly grateful for a second chance.

If you are reading this, it is not too late for you to know Him. Our entrance into the kingdom of heaven comes as we realize our need and turn our hearts toward the cross of Jesus, remembering that He is the King. I encourage you to call out to Him with those six critical words today, "God forgive me. God help me."

Following my return, my life underwent significant changes, each step marked by spiritual enrichment and a renewed sense of purpose. Driven by the encounter with Jesus and His command, I became a messenger of hope, redemption, and the reality of a spiritual existence beyond the physical realm. I embarked on a mission to share my story across the world, emphasizing that the divine light I experienced is accessible to all and that we are all part of a larger, divine tapestry that connects each of us to the heavenly.

Through my testimony, I aim to ignite a flame of faith in others, demonstrating that transformation and redemption are within reach, and that our earthly journey is deeply intertwined with the spiritual path laid out before us. This mission has not only defined my existence but has also offered a beacon of light to those still searching for their way home to spiritual truth and peace.

FURTHER REFLECTION

Jim Woodford's journey challenges us to reconsider our understanding of success and fulfillment. While Jim's life was marked by achievements and adventure, his profound encounter with the divine revealed a deeper truth: the true measure of a life well-lived lies in love, forgiveness, and spiritual connection. This reflection invites us to ponder our own lives. Are we pursuing merely earthly success, or are we seeking a deeper relationship with the divine?

Envision yourself in Jim's place, experiencing the transition from earthly struggles to divine encounters. Reflect on the areas of your life where you may need to seek forgiveness or offer it to others. Contemplate the moments when you felt the presence of something greater guiding you, and ask for the strength to live a life that aligns with this higher calling.

PRAYER

Dear Heavenly Father,

As I reflect on Jim's story, I am reminded of the profound love and mercy You extend to each of us. Help me to see beyond the distractions of this world and to recognize Your guiding hand in my life. Grant me the wisdom to seek forgiveness where it is needed and the courage to offer it to others. May my heart be open to Your presence, leading me toward a life filled with compassion, kindness, and purpose. Guide me on my journey, that I may live in a way that honors You and brings light to those around me. Help me to embrace the spiritual truths revealed through Jim's testimony, and to share Your love and grace with everyone I meet.

Amen.

CHAPTER 2
A MAN WAS TAKEN IN A
TORNADO AND SURVIVED

"Not only so, but we also glory in our sufferings, because we know that suffering produces perseverance; perseverance, character; and character, hope."
- Romans 5:3-4 (NIV)

Jason may be one of the only people who have experienced being taken into the funnel of a tornado and lived to tell about it. Miracles in his testimony also include deliverance from addiction, power of a mother's prayer and redemption. Today Jason is passionate about encouraging others in finding freedom from bondage of any form. I love his heart and his passion for serving others! - Julie

My name is **Jason Miller**. I grew up in a large Amish family with 12 siblings. Growing up Amish taught me a lot about faith and living simply. Those values stuck with me, even when I decided to leave and explore the world beyond. Leaving wasn't easy—I was curious, but I also felt like I was losing a part of myself. Little did I know, the real chaos was still ahead, not in my search for deeper truths, but as I faced the challenges of a looming storm.

At 21, I left the Amish church in search of more. I had a deep longing to find the truth. I began my search and attended many different churches. What I ultimately found was a lot of religion. I was very disappointed. I wanted to find my purpose. I was excommunicated by my community and this drove me further away from all I had known. I always struggled to fit in as a kid. When I left my community I wanted to assimilate to the culture but it was very tough. I was shocked by the crude nature of people. When I opposed it I was ridiculed. It was very hurtful.

Although I had great morals and a strong work ethic, this culture conflict led me to start drinking. I knew nothing about addiction. Slowly things spiraled. Someone I thought was a friend led me to drugs and over several years I was heading on a path toward destruction. In retrospect I know that I opened a spiritual door to the demonic in my life. I didn't know how to shut it. Suddenly my behavior began to change. I felt like I was on a tidal wave out to a sea of darkness. The evening of March 1st, 2012 I was on the phone with my mom desperate and bawling, talking to her about my situation. I was out of control and in an unhealthy relationship. My mom and sister were praying for me.

March 2nd, 2012, began like any other day, marked by the ordinary ebb and flow of life. Yet, the calm of the day was deceptive, a precursor to the chaos that was about to unfold. The forecast hinted at a storm, a common enough occurrence, but nothing could have prepared me for the cataclysm that was about to descend. As the sky darkened and the wind gathered force, a sense of unease took hold. The news confirmed the worst: an EF 4 tornado, with wind speeds around 175 mph, was barreling its way not far from our location.

In the moments before the tornado struck, I faced what felt like the embodiment of death itself as I opened my door to find the tornado changing course, heading straight for my home. The panic and screams of my neighbors echoed my own fear, yet amidst the chaos, a profound desire to protect them took root within me. I grabbed their little girl Angel, and they grabbed their other children, and we fled to my larger home. I led them, a family of five, to what I believed was the safest part of my house.

After I shut the door, I ran and threw myself on top of them in the middle of the home. We were all praying and screaming. There was panic but it didn't last long. We could actually feel the house move on the foundation.

The air grew heavy, as if sucked out of the room, followed by the sound of an explosion, shattering glass and our collective prayers. I blacked out. Inside the funnel of the tornado, there was a moment of eerie awareness, a fleeting instance where the chaos of the storm seemed to pause. I remember being enveloped by the deafening roar, an almost surreal sensation of being lifted and carried away, as if detached from the reality of what was happening. This brief memory is etched in my mind. I am told that I woke up in a field with amnesia roughly a quarter of a mile away from my home. Witnesses report that I was walking but badly injured.

Miraculously, I was one of a few people in history to survive a tornado that powerful, but not without a litany of injuries—multiple fractures, including my spine, and extensive damage to my arm. Hearing about my friends not surviving, through a news report in the hospital added a whole new layer of pain. Little Angel was on life support for a time but did not survive. I was heartbroken to hear this news and plagued by the what ifs.

Lying in the hospital, grappling with both physical and emotional scars, a divine epiphany struck me. God clearly helped me see that the power of my mother's prayers had been instrumental in saving my life. This realization was not merely a source of comfort but a profound revelation of the tangible power of prayer, a testament to the unseen forces at work, guided by a mother's unwavering faith. I was so grateful, but there was much healing that would need to take place. Hearing so many people with good intent tell me God must have some special purpose for me after losing my friends was very hard to hear at that time.

The aftermath of the tornado plunged me into a dark spiral of depression, addiction, crime, and even homelessness. It was a descent into despair, a journey marked by the struggle to find meaning and purpose in the wake of such devastation. Yet, it was also during this time that the most powerful aspect of my journey unfolded. Through the kindness of strangers and pivotal moments of clarity, I found myself on a path to healing, discovering a relationship with the Holy Spirit I never knew possible.

At my lowest, when hope seemed a distant memory, it was Jesus who helped me piece together the fragments of my life.

One of the things God did while I was in rehab that I will never forget involved sensing two angels around a man. I was in a church when I saw two distinguished men enter. They were dressed in suits. One of the men stood out to me. Somehow I saw in the spirit that there were two huge warrior angels walking with one of these men. I knew they were protecting this man from something. During the service I felt the Lord was prompting me to tell this man what I saw. I am in a rehab and only a few months sober, and this man is very well-to-do and I felt hesitant to approach him, yet the nudge continued. He got up and walked out immediately after the service. I was nervous, but I followed him and shared with him what God had shown me. He seemed a little surprised but he didn't say a word. He turned and walked away.

Several weeks later I am at the same church, this same man is standing at the front of the church. When he sees me, he runs toward me and is very excited to share some news. He explained that he is a business owner. The day I first saw him, he discovered that his wife was cheating on him with his best friend. She was going to divorce him and take half of the business. He had given up on God but his friend insisted on taking him to church that night. He told God he would go, but if God didn't show up in some way that he was going to take his life. When I stopped him and shared about the angels, he knew immediately that God was watching over him. God used me, a struggling kid in rehab, to bless this man!

This journey, fraught with trials, taught me the invaluable lesson that there is always hope, regardless of the circumstances, because of God's redemptive power, grace, and love. The trials I endured were not merely obstacles but opportunities for growth, shaping my character and resilience, preparing me for a new purpose. Today, I stand as an entrepreneur, a vocal political advocate in my community, driven by a desire to offer encouragement to those in despair. My message is one of unwavering hope in God's ability to transform lives. Through every trial, God has been refining me, equipping me with strength, character, and perseverance for a calling far greater than I could have imagined. I feel God spared me for His purposes.

My story is a testament to the enduring strength of faith and the reality that, even in our darkest moments, God is working to bring about redemption and renewal. For anyone struggling, know that there is true hope in God, a hope that can carry you through the storm and lead you to a place of strength and purpose.

FURTHER REFLECTION

Jason's journey underscores the power of faith, prayer, and divine intervention. His experiences show that even in the darkest times, God's presence and guidance can lead to profound transformation and renewal. From surviving a devastating tornado to overcoming addiction and finding purpose, Jason's life is a testament to God's redemptive power. His life encourages us to trust in God, even when circumstances seem insurmountable, and to remain open to the ways God can work through our lives.

Reflect on your own challenges and consider how faith has played a role in your journey. Think about the power of prayer and how it has influenced your life. How can you deepen your trust in God and remain open to His guidance and intervention? Remember that even in the most difficult moments, God is working to bring about redemption and renewal in your life.

PRAYER

Lord,

Thank You for Your unwavering presence and the transformative power of Your love. Help us to trust in Your guidance and remain open to Your will, even in the face of adversity. Strengthen our faith and remind us of the power of prayer. May we find hope and purpose in Your plan for our lives, and may we be a source of encouragement and inspiration to others.

Amen.

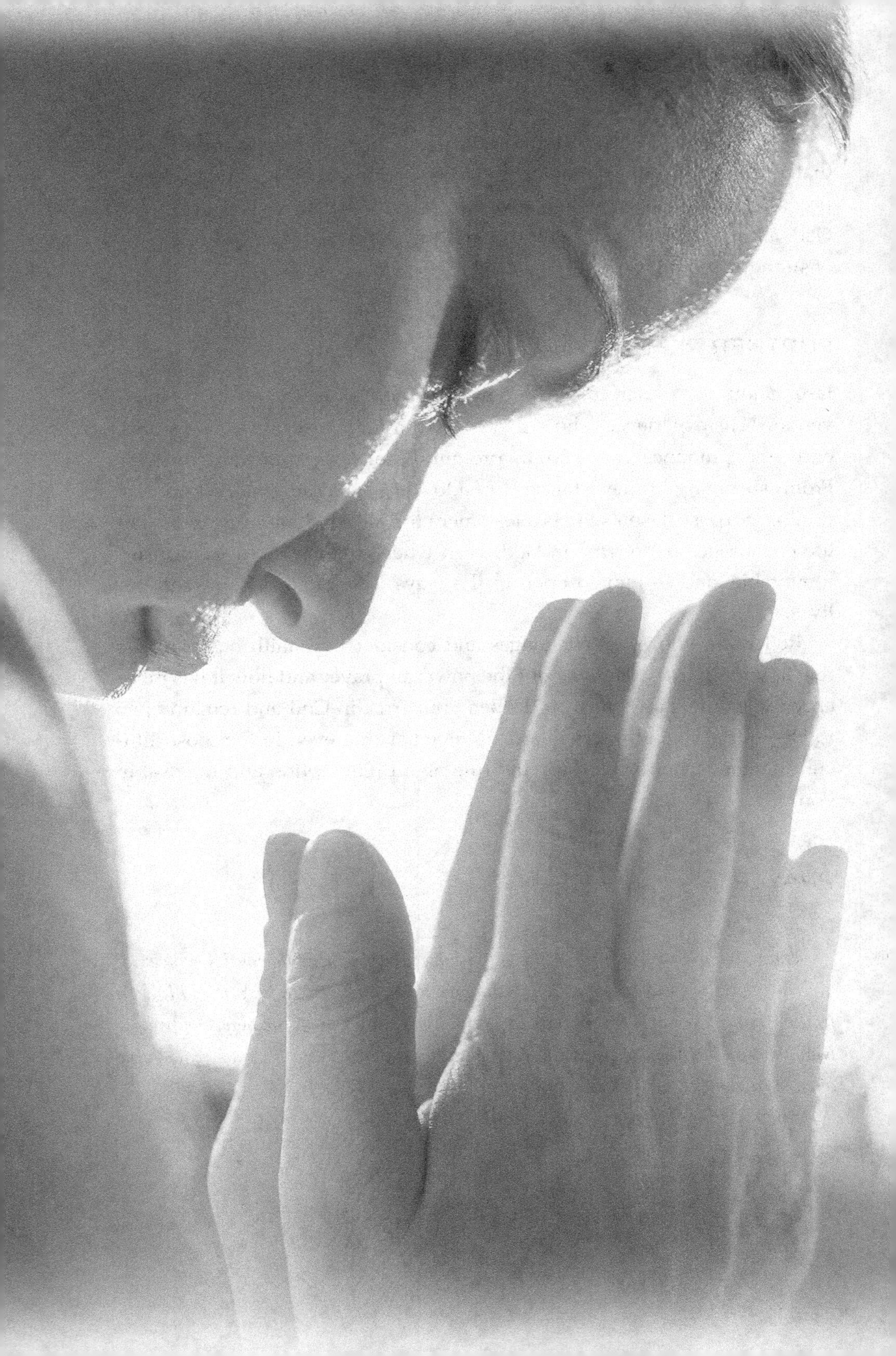

CHAPTER 3
A HEALING EVANGELIST WITNESSES THE MIRACULOUS

"And these signs will accompany those who believe: In my name they will drive out demons; they will speak in new tongues...they will place their hands on sick people, and they will get well."
- Mark 16:17-18 (NIV)

Joan has personally experienced the miraculous healing power of God and has spent most of her life serving the Lord and equipping other believers in healing ministry. She has uncompromising faith and dedication to the call of God on her life. She exhibits a sincere desire to see the body of Christ set free in their body, mind, soul, spirit and finances. Joan Hunter is a compassionate minister, dynamic teacher, an accomplished author, and an anointed healing evangelist. She is the TV show host of "Miracles Happen!" in Tomball, TX. I am inspired by her obedience and dedication to Jesus and love her warm and down-to-earth personality! - Julie

I am **Joan Hunter**. My story begins with my birth under extremely difficult circumstances. My mother married a man who, on their wedding night, tried to kill her. He was the man God used to bring me here. His actions set the stage for the trauma I experienced from conception. My mother ran for her life, and later, for ours. She was a tough woman, raised me with a sailor's mouth, drank martinis like water, and smoked heavily. This was the environment I grew up in.

When I was about 12, my mother underwent a radical transformation. A persistent pastor, despite my mother's harsh lifestyle, managed to show her the love of God. One morning, I woke up to a completely different mother. She had quit smoking, drinking, and swearing overnight. This change in her led me to give my heart to Jesus within about 30 days. From that moment on, I never turned back.

At 16, my mother met Charles Hunter in Texas, where they had a whirlwind romance and got married 88 days later. By the time I was 18, I was traveling with them, engaging in ministry work. This marked the beginning of my 53-year journey in healing ministry. After high school, I went to Oral Roberts University and later got married. My marriage lasted 25 years, during which we had four daughters. However, it ended when I discovered my husband was living a double life in an alternative lifestyle. This revelation was devastating, but God released me to get a divorce.

The aftermath of my divorce was challenging. I was diagnosed with breast cancer, which I believe was rooted in unresolved emotional trauma. Shortly after, I was also diagnosed with broken heart syndrome, a condition that can be fatal. In my despair, I cried out to God, seeking healing. I experienced a profound spiritual cleansing in the shower one day, where I let go of all unforgiveness, bitterness, and abandonment issues. Miraculously, my breast cancer disappeared, confirmed by subsequent medical tests. God also healed my broken heart syndrome supernaturally!

Although it was not easy to experience these hardships, God revealed so much to me about healing and the authority we carry as followers of Jesus (Luke 10:19). The Bible is clear about His will for us to be healed. Every single believer has a healing ministry. Perhaps it is not traveling all over the world. I asked God once why He picked a 70-year-old woman like me to do this work. His answer was, **"Because you said yes, and you meant it."**

I can still remember the first time I was asked to participate in healing prayer alongside my parents. I was very involved with my parents' ministry and always eager to help behind the scenes as needed. We were ministering in a large school gymnasium. They wanted to set up four lines for healing prayer. For the first time I was directed to take a group. "Take them where?" I asked. They set me up on the stage to pray. I was reluctant, but obediently began to pray just as I had watched my parents, and in the name of Jesus. Several people came through my line when suddenly I heard screaming. I stopped to see if someone got hurt or needed help. Suddenly a woman exclaims, "I was blind and now I can see!" My shocked response, "Are you kidding?!" God can work through you if you are obedient and willing.

Throughout my life and ministry, I have witnessed countless miracles. People have been healed from blindness, limb regrowth, arthritis, and migraines, among other ailments. I emphasize the power of forgiveness and breaking soul ties, which are often the spiritual roots of physical ailments. Trauma is also a very important and common issue that we must address through prayer. We can also pray and ask God to erase our painful memories (Philippians 3:13). I have written over 27 books, conducted numerous healing services, and taught many about the authority we have as believers to lay hands on the sick and see them recover.

One unique aspect of my ministry is the use of prayer blankets. These blankets, which I have prayed over, have been instrumental in bringing healing to many people. From brain-dead patients recovering to veterans finding peace from PTSD, the testimonies are endless. These blankets carry the anointing of God and have shown miraculous results in various situations. We find this practice in the Bible in Acts 19:12, where Paul's healing anointing from Jesus was so strong that contact with some of his articles of clothing were used to heal people of their sickness and evil spirits.

In my journey, I have learned the importance of listening to God's prompting. Whether it is praying for someone in a store or on a plane, God's healing power is always ready to be manifested. One memorable incident was praying for a man with severe diabetes at the Liberty Bell.

Despite the circumstances, God healed him right there as he continued his job. Even a quick prayer in Jesus' name is enough to see someone get healed.

As believers, we must be aware of our spiritual authority and exercise it. Jesus left us with all His authority, and it is our responsibility to use it. In my ministry, I train others to understand this authority and to use it to bring healing to those around them.

Looking back, I am amazed at how God has used me, a 70-year-old woman, to travel the world and bring His healing power to many. It is a testament to saying yes to God and meaning it. God has a plan for each of us, and when we step out in faith, He uses us in extraordinary ways.

I encourage everyone to speak life over themselves and others, to forgive, and to trust in God's healing power. My journey has not been easy, but it has been filled with God's miracles and His undeniable presence. May God bless you and heal you as you seek Him with all your heart.

FURTHER REFLECTION

Joan Hunter's journey reveals the transformative power of faith, forgiveness, and obedience to God. Her story reminds us that even amidst profound challenges, healing and miracles are within reach for those who trust in God's power. Reflect on the moments in your life where you have experienced hardship and consider how faith and forgiveness could bring healing to those wounds. Are you open to being used by God, regardless of your age or circumstances?

Imagine yourself in Joan's position, experiencing profound changes and witnessing miracles. How can you apply the lessons of faith and authority in your own life? Ask God to show you areas where you can step out in faith and be a vessel for His healing and love.

PRAYER

Dear Heavenly Father,

Thank You for the powerful testimony of Joan Hunter and the miracles You have worked through her life. Help me to embrace the faith and authority You have given me as Your follower. Teach me to forgive and to let go of any bitterness or hurt that may hinder my spiritual growth. Guide me to step out in faith, trusting in Your power to bring healing and restoration to those around me. Strengthen my resolve to listen to Your prompting and to be obedient to Your call, no matter the circumstances. May I be a beacon of Your love and healing in this world, always ready to serve and minister to those in need. I ask for Your guidance and courage as I seek to live a life that glorifies You.

Amen.

CHAPTER 4
BEYOND HEAVEN'S GATE: A JOURNEY TO HEAVEN AND BACK

"For I am persuaded that neither death nor life, nor angels nor principalities nor powers, nor things present nor things to come, nor height nor depth, nor any other created thing, shall be able to separate us from the love of God which is in Christ Jesus our Lord."
- Romans 8:38-39 (NKJV)

Dean Braxton was clinically dead for one hour and 45 minutes, only to come fully back to life! Even more stunning is what he experienced during this time in the presence of Jesus. Dean is the joy of the Lord personified. He is one of the most passionate and Spirit-filled people I have been honored to interview. He is spreading the love of Jesus around the globe through books, speaking, and ministry and bringing many to know Jesus as their personal Lord and Savior! - Julie

I 'm **Dean Braxton**, years ago, I found myself in a situation that, medically speaking, I shouldn't have survived. I went to the hospital for what seemed like a routine procedure to treat kidney stones—a condition painful but not usually life-threatening. However, things took a turn for the worse when an infection led to sepsis, causing my organs to fail one by one. Before I knew it, I was on the brink of death.

I was clinically dead for an hour and 45 minutes. To the healthcare professionals who witnessed my condition, my survival, let alone without any deficits, was nothing short of miraculous. They even started calling me the "Miracle Man." But behind this miracle was a profound spiritual journey that would redefine the essence of my faith and purpose.

Let me tell you, the realization that you're dying is a profound moment. As I was wheeled down to the ICU, struggling for every breath, a sense of peace enveloped me. It was a peace that made no sense in the natural realm, given my circumstances. I had always feared dying, especially in a manner that involved suffocation, given a childhood experience with almost drowning. Yet, in that moment, all fear was replaced by an overwhelming sense of joy and anticipation. I was going home.

I remember leaving the hospital room. I remember leaving the atmosphere. I remember leaving what we call our universe. I remember entering this dark area. Many people say they could see a light at the end of the tunnel. I saw a light and it looked like a window. And I was headed toward it. And I knew that's where the father of Jesus is. Somehow I knew that was heaven. Suddenly, as I continued moving, these other lights were passing me by like I was standing still. They looked like shooting stars. They weren't, but that's what they looked like. And they were the prayers that people were praying for me and others.

It was a very joyful moment for me seeing them go past. Later on when I was processing that whole scene, I wondered why the prayers were going faster than I was. And I was going really fast, and yet it looked like the prayers were passing me so much faster. All I could really see was the ends of them or the tails. Very similar to a shooting star up in the sky, you see the tail.

The whole experience was beyond any human words could describe. The journey there wasn't just about moving from one place to another; it was an immediate transition into a state of being enveloped in love, peace, and a profound sense of rightness. Everything was as it should be, and I was exactly where I was meant to be. For the first time, I felt like I fit perfectly in this beautiful place! I wish I could grab the feeling at that moment and give it away to everybody I come in contact with, to have that total feeling of fitting in a place.

In heaven, my meeting with Jesus and the Father was life-changing. It wasn't just like seeing someone; it was more like being wrapped up in the deepest sense of love and peace you can imagine. I bowed before Him, at His feet in awe, "You did this for me!" This realization that my presence in heaven was solely due to His sacrifice was overwhelming. Our meeting was deeply personal, reflecting love and acceptance. Initially I could only look at His feet. The fullness of the love of God was coming through the feet of Jesus. I don't know how else to say it, but every portion of His being that I looked at loved me. I could feel the love emanating through His feet, ankles, knees, and the marks of His crucifixion, I understood that His identity was unmistakable through this boundless love. Indeed, as Romans 8 declares, nothing can separate us from God's love, a truth made evident through Christ.

This love is great and it's expanding every moment. I wish we could understand that we're wired for that love. We're created for that love. The reason you were created is because God just wants to be with you. You're created because God Almighty wants to be with you forever. He has already chosen us. He just wants us to choose Him. When I looked into His eyes, what did I see? I saw the love for myself. And then I thought about somebody else and I saw the love for them. If I would have known you back then and thought about you, I would have seen the love for you like you're the only one He loves. I remember saying later on, "You really do want everybody here."

Then I made a statement because I worked in the juvenile justice system for many years. I worked for kids who were abused. I remember we could deal with everything. But when we had a kid that had been sexually abused, boy, that was hard to deal with. Could those people really be changed when they came into the love of God? In my mind, I was thinking about that abuser many times, and it wasn't that I didn't think God would not forgive them, but I always had him in the back of the line.

When I experienced this love I questioned, "Even child molesters?" He's still looking away, but he started to make a statement. He says,

"When you put a person in jail, they get out. They get out because their time's up, or they die, but they get out."

And then he turned around and looked at me. He's looking down, and He says, "But when we put a person in hell, they are there for eternity." He says, "Who are you to nullify what I have done?" You know, and at that moment, it hit me. He's the one that died on the cross.

In Isaiah 52 it says He was beaten in such a manner He was unrecognizable as a human being. He paid the price for everybody. So I have no right to say this person cannot be saved by God. I'm not saying they're not going to pay the price on the planet for their wrongdoing, but I am going to say if they ask God to forgive them, God's going to forgive them.

I know some of us, we're going to have a hard time with that because we want some people to really pay forever, but Jesus Christ died on the cross for everyone.

One of the things Jesus was doing when I got there was very interesting. He was facing a bunch of beings or angels out in front of them, and they were in a half circle. He was communicating with them, and I knew what He was doing. He was strategizing. He was strategizing around how to get people on the planet to know Jesus Christ as Lord and Savior. He was coming up with these strategies because people were praying, and as they were praying for loved ones, Jesus Almighty up in heaven was strategizing with the angels to orchestrate events on the planet to get people born again.

The angels weren't giving Him advice. He was directing everything. The strategy wasn't so much on the angels. They were going to do what they needed to do in the heavenly realm. It was really on the planet. Who on the planet He could rely on to do what He wanted to be done. And I came to understand He was strategizing beyond individuals. He was also looking at churches. He wasn't looking at just the Baptists or the Methodists or the Pentecostals, He was looking at churches that were following Him. It didn't matter what denomination. If they were following Him, He was using them in the strategy.

You know, He told me that in every church, there's really two types of spirits and two types of attitude. He said that one was like the church of Philadelphia, if you read Revelation, and the other one is like the church of

Laodicea. He said that kind of personality or attitude is in every church. One time you may go to a church and it looks like more of them are following what Laodicea did. And you go to another church and more of them are following what Philadelphia did. It did not matter what denomination it was, He was moving them in their position in their community to work out His will on the planet.

One of the most profound insights from this journey was a family reunion. I was warmly welcomed by a huge family reunion that included many generations, even those from way before my time. It showed me how family ties go on forever, kept strong by God's love. It made me see how special family connections are, lasting way beyond our time on Earth. I learned that in heaven, we get to work and celebrate together with our families, which was a really comforting thought. It reassured me that the relationships we value so much here are not just for now, but forever.

In reference to family, there are four groups that come to greet you into heaven: your family, your friends, anyone you led to the Lord, and yes, your pets. Pets in heaven are often controversial. I didn't believe animals went to heaven when this happened to me. Here I am on my hands and knees before Jesus looking at His feet. To my side, here come all these pets, animals. I prayed to God in the hospital that no one would ask me about pets in heaven. Of course, they did. As I poured into the Bible I found several scriptures that speak to their place in God's Kingdom.

I had more encounters with Jesus, but ultimately He told me that it was not yet my time and that I had to go back. I wanted so much to stay in this place. I felt He was saying to me that He needed me more on the Earth. In spite of my disappointment, the words arose in me, like a soldier, "Yes Sir." I felt myself going back in the opposite direction, and I saw the prayers flying toward heaven once again. I cried all the way to my hospital bed. Three days later I woke up.

As they removed the breathing tube, the first words that escaped my lips were, "There's a Jesus. You don't have to hope there's a Jesus. You don't have to wish there was a Jesus. There's a Jesus," While I longed to stay in that place of absolute peace and love, I was sent back with a purpose. Since then, I've been on a mission to share this experience, to tell others about the reality of Jesus, the power of prayer, and the tangible love of God that transcends our earthly understanding.

My wife's role in my survival and recovery cannot be overstated. She was a warrior of faith, leading a prayer battle that I believe was pivotal in my miraculous recovery. She maintained a spiritual atmosphere around me, one that fostered healing and divine intervention. Her unwavering belief in God's power and her strategic prayers were instrumental in what many would call a comeback from the dead.

After my return, I was reading the Bible. God gave me more revelation about the prayers that were passing me so quickly on my way to heaven. I was reading in Genesis when it was just Adam and God. There was no one else for Adam to talk to in the beginning. And then I got it. Why wouldn't the prayers pass me by? God wants so much to hear from us. He loves it when we communicate with Him. He loves your voice. He made your voice. He created you to talk to Him and to hear from Him. Remember that prayers don't have a shelf life. Those that are coming from your heart. They do not expire. I realized that in the Bible, in a story about Cornelius when an angel comes to Him and says to Him, "Your prayers and your good deeds are memorial before God." The word *memorial* in Greek means "remembrance." I tell people so often that they are blessed. You're praying and interceding. There are so many generations ago that also interceded for their family, and God is still blessing them because of those prayers!

The impact of this journey on my life has been monumental. It's transformed how I view every moment, every interaction, and every challenge. Knowing what awaits us, understanding the depth of God's love, and realizing the importance of our time here on Earth has fueled my passion to live a life that reflects this love and to share the hope that comes from knowing Jesus.

As I share my story, I'm often met with skepticism, curiosity, and sometimes, a deep sense of longing for that same assurance of what lies beyond this life. To those who doubt, I offer my testimony not as proof but as a witness to the power of faith. To those who seek, I say, keep your heart open to the possibilities of God's love and the reality of His kingdom.

Reflecting on the past 18 years fills me with immense gratitude for the opportunities I've been given to share my testimony and minister in 15 different countries. My journey has led me through a wide range of places, from civil clubs and business meetings to encounters with political figures, inmates, the Amish, new-age enthusiasts, and even witches. The privilege of bringing Jesus' light into churches, schools, outdoor gatherings, hospitals, and intimate family settings has been a profound blessing. Whether speaking at daycares or colleges, participating in funerals, or comforting those at life's threshold, each moment has been a testament to the power of faith, hope, and love to transcend all boundaries.

FURTHER REFLECTION

Dean Braxton's incredible experience challenges us to recognize the profound love and peace that awaits us in heaven. His testimony emphasizes the power of prayer, the reality of Jesus' love, and the eternal significance of our relationships. Reflect on the depth of God's love and how it can transform fear into peace and doubt into faith. Consider the impact of your prayers and the assurance that they are heard and cherished by God.

Imagine yourself standing before Jesus, enveloped in His boundless love. What fears or burdens can you release into His care? How can you deepen your prayer life, knowing that your words reach the heart of God and have the power to change lives?

PRAYER

Dear Heavenly Father,

Thank You for the inspiring testimony of Dean Braxton and the profound love he experienced. Help me to embrace the reality of Your love and to trust in the power of prayer. Guide me to live a life that reflects Your love, peace, and compassion. Strengthen my faith, and help me to release my fears and burdens into Your care. May I always remember that my prayers are heard and valued by You. Teach me to intercede for others with a heart full of faith and hope. Guide me to be a vessel of Your love and grace in the world, bringing light to those in darkness and hope to those in despair.

Amen.

CHAPTER 5
FROM TRAFFICKED TO TRIUMPHANT

"The LORD is close to the brokenhearted
and saves those who are crushed in spirit."
- Psalm 34:18 (NIV)

Rebecca's testimony includes miracles of deliverance, healing, and redemption. A high school varsity athlete, she was planning for college when life took an unexpected turn. Circumstances led her into a trap set by a trafficker, where she was exploited for six years in Las Vegas. Jesus met Rebecca in her deepest heartache. He has redeemed her life in the most spectacular way and is using her today in ways she could have never dreamed. Today Rebecca's Elevate Academy is the largest online program for survivors of human trafficking in the world. She was appointed to the U.S. National Advisory Council and regularly testifies as an expert witness in court. Her specialized training has equipped well over 100,000 professionals including FBI, Homeland Security, regional law enforcement, community leaders, and medical personnel. A highly sought-after speaker, consultant, and nationally recognized authority, Rebecca is passionate about seeing people trans-

form their lives! She humbly gives all the glory to God, and I love that.
- Julie

I am **Rebecca Bender**, and this is my story, a journey from vulnerability and trafficking to redemption and advocacy. Growing up in a small town, I was your typical high school girl with dreams and aspirations, deeply influenced by a family environment that lacked a strong faith foundation. My parents' divorce and the subsequent feelings of neglect sowed seeds of vulnerability that would later be exploited. Despite these challenges, I graduated high school early, filled with ambition and plans to attend Oregon State University to pursue architecture. However, life took an unexpected turn when I became pregnant, leading me to sacrifice my college dreams to stay in my small town.

The encounter that drastically altered the course of my life was meeting a man who seemed to offer everything I longed for: attention, care for my daughter, and the semblance of a family. What I couldn't see was that this relationship was a trap set by a trafficker. My naivety and the deep-seated desire for belonging led me into a world of exploitation I had no framework to understand. Contrary to the common narratives of trafficking involving kidnapping and chains, my experience was one of gradual boundary pushing and emotional manipulation, making it difficult to recognize the reality of my situation. Before I knew it, I was entangled in the dark and dangerous world of trafficking in Las Vegas. For nearly six years, I was brainwashed, trapped, and subjected to violence, traded and sold like property.

My turning point came through a deeply personal and transformative encounter at a Christian rehab, where I was introduced to a faith that I had never known. It was here that I experienced radical salvation and heard God's voice for the first time. During my prayer time, I had a memory of sitting alone on the floor in my kitchen, beaten after being hit by my trafficker. I remember slumping to the floor, wiping the blood from my face, and thinking, *"Why won't he love me? What more can I do to make him love me? I've done everything he has asked. I have endured all of this awfulness. Why won't he love me?"* That is the moment when the Lord spoke to me, "That's how I feel about you. What more can *I* do? I died on the cross. I've given

My blood for you. What more can I do to make you love Me?" I just remember feeling heartbroken for Jesus. I didn't realize I could grieve the heart of God. It was a real epiphany in my walk with the Lord. This pivotal moment began my journey of healing and a profound relationship with God, opening my eyes to a purpose and destiny beyond my circumstances.

My recovery was not just about overcoming substance abuse or escaping my trafficker; it was about finding my voice and a sense of purpose through my faith. Engaging with law enforcement and sharing my story publicly, despite the fears and potential risks, became part of my mission to combat trafficking and support other survivors. Through this work, I've come to understand the power of my story not just as a tale of survival, but as a testament to the transformative love and redemption offered by God.

My life's work is dedicated to combating human trafficking, supporting survivors, and educating the public about this pervasive issue. Through my advocacy, I aim to contribute to a world where exploitation is recognized and combated, and where survivors find the support and healing they need to reclaim their lives. My journey from a victim of trafficking to an advocate for change is a testament to the power of faith, the strength of the human spirit, and the boundless capacity for renewal and hope.

FURTHER REFLECTION

Rebecca Bender's journey highlights the transformative power of faith and the profound impact of God's love. Her story reminds us that no matter how deep our struggles, redemption and purpose are always within reach. Reflect on the moments in your life where you felt lost or vulnerable, and consider how embracing faith could bring healing and new direction. Are there areas in your life where you need to trust in God's love and allow it to transform you?

Imagine yourself in Rebecca's position, feeling God's profound love and hearing His call. How can you respond to God's love in your own life? What steps can you take to deepen your faith and share His love with others?

PRAYER

Dear Heavenly Father,

Thank You for the powerful testimony of Rebecca Bender and the incredible transformation she experienced through Your love. Help me to recognize the areas in my life where I need Your healing touch. Grant me the courage to trust in Your love and to embrace the purpose You have for me. Guide me to be a beacon of hope and support to those who are struggling, and use my life to bring awareness and change to the issues that burden our world. Strengthen my faith and help me to walk confidently in the path You have laid out for me, knowing that Your love is always with me.

Amen

CHAPTER 6
JESUS APPEARS AND ORCHESTRATES A SUPERNATURAL RESCUE

"And He said to me, 'My grace is sufficient for you, for My strength is made perfect in weakness.' Therefore most gladly I will rather boast in my infirmities, that the power of Christ may rest upon me_."
- 2 Corinthians 12:9 (NKJV)

"Sheila's life was forever changed the night she was in a tragic accident. Jesus appeared on the scene and orchestrated a supernatural rescue that would trigger a ripple effect of miracles and lead her to a deeply personal relationship with Him. Her testimony of struggle and perseverance has inspired people of all age groups and walks of life. God has led her to write, speak and minister on various topics including limb loss, trauma, and hope. Sheila radiates the light and love of Jesus to every person in her path!" - Julie

I am **Sheila Preston Fitzgerald**, and I want to share a testimony that reshaped my entire existence, a journey from a mere "check the box" Christian to experiencing the profound depth of God's love and the reality of Jesus Christ in a way that words can barely capture. My story isn't just about an event; it's about transformation, a divine intervention that redefined everything I thought I knew about faith, survival, and the power of prayer.

Several years ago, I found myself in a life-threatening motorcycle accident. My husband and I, both avid riders, were returning from a dinner with friends, fully geared up for safety. As I entered a major intersection, with the light green and my right of way clear, an unforeseen calamity unfolded. An SUV abruptly pulled in front of me, followed too closely by a sedan that left me with no escape. In that split second, my world forever changed. My motorcycle crashed into the car, pinning my left leg, and catapulting me into the air with such force that when I landed, my right side took the brunt of the impact. My helmet came off, and there I was, lying on the pavement, conscious and overwhelmed by the heightened sensitivity that the trauma induced. Every sound was amplified, every touch was electric, and the smells were overpoweringly vivid. Amidst this chaos, my husband, a fire department officer, rushed to my aid, his training kicking in automatically.

It was in this moment of utter vulnerability and pain that something extraordinary happened. Lying there, fearing I might be paralyzed, thoughts of my brother, who had lived as a quadriplegic, filled my mind. I couldn't bear the thought of putting my family through that ordeal again. So, I prayed. Not a well-thought-out prayer, but a desperate barter with God. I was ready to surrender my life rather than be a burden. Yet, in that plea for release, I wasn't prepared for the answer I would receive.

Suddenly, amidst the blaring sirens and frantic voices, a peace enveloped me. It was as if the chaos of the scene around me faded into the background, and I found myself in a different presence—divine and loving. I felt a touch on my right forearm, soft yet firm, pulling my attention away from my injuries and fears. Turning my head, I looked directly into the most indescribable eyes, filled with love, acceptance, peace, and comfort. It was Jesus. In that moment, every doubt, every sin, and every failure of mine was laid bare, yet met with unconditional love. Jesus knew me entirely—the depth of my heart, the sins I carried, and the burdens I bore. And still, He loved me.

I was in total awe of Jesus. I admit there was a moment I was thinking,

"Wow! They really do exist!" I considered myself a Christian, but as a human I still fought doubts that Jesus, the Holy Spirit and angels are tanigble and ever present. The atmosphere around us had shifted. It is difficult to put into words, but there was this beautiful and warm color of deep and brilliant blue that seemed to have a diamond dust sheen to it. It felt inviting and full of a peace I had never known. I didn't want to leave. I wanted to stay right there with Jesus and the Holy Spirit.

I was cradled, literally and figuratively, in the lap of God, surrounded by a sense of safety and peace that transcends human understanding. This wasn't just a feeling; it was a profound, life-altering experience. Jesus assured me, when He spoke to me, **"Don't be afraid. We've got you. You're going to be okay."** This wasn't a mere platitude; it was a promise from the Divine, and it filled me with an unshakable faith and a peace that has stayed with me ever since.

As Jesus lifted His hand, I thought, *This is it; I'm going to heaven*. But the narrative God had for me was far from over. Just then, the unmistakable sound of Life Flight's blades cutting through the air reached my ears—a helicopter ambulance that arrived as if dispatched by heaven itself. There had been no call made for it, yet there it was, a testament to the miraculous orchestration of my rescue.

The journey from that intersection, to the hospital and through the years of recovery that followed, was punctuated with miracles. My leg, nearly amputated at the scene, was saved by a series of divine interventions and medical expertise at Vanderbilt Hospital.

Some time after the accident, the paramedic on the scene shared that he heard a voice tell him not to straighten out my legs. He denied protocol by following this voice. Once the extent of my injuries were realized, it became clear that straightening my legs would have caused me to bleed out quickly and most likely not survive. There was a fourteen-year-old girl on the scene who was unable to run due to an injury. But God. He gave her legs to run to me. She prayed over me on the scene and was ultimately led to become a nurse practitioner.

The recovery was grueling, marked by multiple surgeries, the battle with a MRSA infection, and the ultimate decision to amputate my leg to save my life. Yet, throughout this harrowing process, my spirit was held aloft by an unbreakable connection to Jesus, forged on the pavement that day.

We all will face times of struggle. We will all have peaks and valleys in life. There is so much to learn even in the dark moments. I lost my leg, I lost my home, I lost some of my friends, and I lost my marriage. While I wouldn't want to go through these things again, I would not trade any of it. The lessons I have learned in the dark moments of struggle are priceless. Those places are where the Lord meets us. When we cry out to Him, He will meet us. Remember that He knew you before you were born. He chose you before you were born. He loves you. He is with you.

As I recovered from the head trauma, someone suggested that I get a children's Bible. This was so helpful. I began to read the scriptures out loud and my relationship with God began to grow once again. When in a trial, it is important to express the emotions of what you are experiencing. First, take it to God in prayer. He can handle whatever you are feeling and expressing. Leaning into Him and into scripture is paramount. I also have developed a love for journaling. This is a great way to start processing your experience and facilitate healing.

One of the lowest moments for me was the day the doctors thought I had bone cancer in my longer leg. I was all alone. I had no family around me. After getting the news I made it to my car and I lost it. Up until that point I was always asking, "How, Lord, are we going to do this?" But at that moment, I was mad that I wasn't taken in the accident. I had to express that anger and let it out and take it to Him. Finding healthy avenues to ventilate your emotions is extremely important.

This encounter with Jesus transformed my faith from a passive, checkbox Christianity to a vibrant, living relationship with God. It taught me the power of prayer, the reality of Jesus' presence, and the profound depth of His love for us. Even in our darkest moments, when we feel most alone and vulnerable, He is there, waiting to cradle us in His peace and assure us of His unending love.

To anyone feeling lost, burdened, or in pain, know this: Jesus is real, His love is unfathomable, and He is always present, ready to transform your pain into purpose, your fears into faith. My journey from the brink of death to a life filled with hope and anchored in Jesus' promise is a testament to His grace, a grace available to all who seek Him.

FURTHER REFLECTION

Sheila Preston Fitzgerald's journey from a devastating motorcycle accident to a profound encounter with Jesus reminds us that even in our darkest moments, God's presence is unwavering. Her story emphasizes the importance of moving beyond a superficial faith to a deep, personal relationship with Jesus. Reflect on the challenges in your life and consider how you can invite God's presence into those struggles. Are there areas where you need to trust more deeply in His love and guidance?

Imagine yourself in Sheila's place, feeling the peace and love of Jesus in your moment of greatest need. How can you cultivate that same sense of connection and trust in your daily life? What steps can you take to deepen your faith and experience God's transformative love?

PRAYER

Dear Heavenly Father,

Thank You for the powerful testimony of Sheila Preston Fitzgerald and the profound love she experienced in her darkest moment. Help me to move beyond a superficial faith and into a deeper, more personal relationship with You. Teach me to trust in Your presence and love, even in my most challenging times. Guide me to lean into Your Word and to express my emotions honestly in prayer. Strengthen my faith and help me to see Your hand at work in every aspect of my life. May Your peace and love fill my heart, transforming my fears into faith and my pain into purpose.

Amen.

CHAPTER 7
JESUS SAVED MY SON FROM DROWNING

"These things I have spoken to you, that in Me you may have peace. In the world you will have tribulation; but be of good cheer, I have overcome the world."
- John 16:33 (NKJV)

Courtney's powerful share reveals the tangible presence of Jesus in so many ways! As a mother and a nurse she experiences the unimaginable battle for the life of her own child. An inexplicable prompting for prayer, the faith of a young praying brother at the scene, the family of providers who faithfully rushed in for support, and Max sharing his encounter with Jesus and what he observed. Praising God with this family for their miracle and for a very present Savior! -Julie

I am **Courtney McKee**, and I want to share with you a miracle that has profoundly impacted my family, a testimony of faith, hope, and a miraculous encounter that we experienced with my youngest son, Max. This journey begins with a regular summer day that turned into an event that would forever change our lives and deepen our faith in ways we never imagined possible.

I'm a mother of two incredible boys, Brody, who is now 11, and Max, the baby of our family at 6 years old. My husband and I, high school sweethearts, blessed with our careers and our precious sons, never foresaw the trials and the miraculous events that were about to unfold. Our story takes a significant turn on July 11th, 2019, a day etched in my memory with both fear and awe.

On that day, wanting to escape the routine and enjoy the warmth of summer, my boys were set to spend some time at my mother's farm, a place of many cherished memories, including afternoons at the pool. It was a scene we envisioned filled with laughter and joy, reminiscent of my own childhood. However, as we dropped them off, a sudden, unexplainable urge to pray overtook me. I asked my husband to stop the car, and there, in the parking lot, we prayed fervently for the protection of our children and my mother. This intense moment of prayer was a prelude to the events that were to unfold.

The following day, amidst a busy shift at the hospital where I work as a nurse, I received a heart-stopping call. My sister-in-law informed me that Max had been found at the bottom of the pool. The details were blurry; how long he had been underwater was uncertain. At that moment, my world came crashing down. The professional environment I was part of, filled with nurses, doctors, and therapists, suddenly became a backdrop to my personal crisis. I couldn't stand; I couldn't speak. My colleagues quickly became my support, enveloping me in prayer and taking charge to ensure Max received the best possible care.

Max's accident was a parent's worst nightmare. He was only two years and ten months old, and after a moment of tiredness from playing, he slipped into the pool unnoticed, his absence was discovered only moments later but moments that felt like an eternity. My sister-in-law, reacting swiftly, pulled him out and started resuscitation efforts while my mother dialed for an ambulance. Amidst this chaos, Brody, my eldest, became a pillar of faith. He knelt and prayed unceasingly for his brother's recovery, a testament to the power of faith we had instilled in our children.

The initial prognosis was dire. Max was lifeless when found, and the uncertainty of how long he had been underwater loomed large. Rushed to the local trauma center, I was caught between my role as a nurse and a mother. I knew the medical steps being taken, the gravity of his condition, yet, as a mother, I felt helpless. My colleagues, my work family, stepped in when I couldn't. They were my voice, advocating for Max, and ensuring he received immediate and comprehensive care.

Seeing Max in the emergency room, surrounded by medical staff, tubes, and machines, was an image I'll never forget. Yet, in that moment of overwhelming fear, my faith never wavered. I prayed, not with words, for I had none, but with my heart, pleading with God to spare my son, to breathe life back into him. It was a prayer of desperation, a cry from the soul of a mother facing the possible loss of her child.

Miraculously, Max's condition began to improve significantly. The prayers of our community, our family, friends, and even strangers, became a powerful force. Max, once on the brink of death, was now recovering at an astonishing rate. He was talking, eager to leave the hospital bed, a testament to the power of faith and prayer.

But the most remarkable part of Max's story was yet to come. After we brought him home, he shared with us an experience that would forever change our understanding of God's presence in our lives. Max told us that he wasn't scared when he was in the water because Jesus held him. He described Jesus' hands, asking about the "boo-boo's and scratches," the marks he saw. "Who hurt him?" he expressed with care and concern. This revelation was astounding. We had never spoken to him about the crucifixion in such detail. His experience, his calm assurance that Jesus was with him, brought indescribable peace to our hearts.

Max's story has since become a beacon of hope for many, especially for parents grieving the loss of a child or grappling with fear and trauma. Hearing a child affirm that they were not alone, that they felt no fear because they were in the arms of Jesus, offers a comfort that words alone cannot provide.

In the aftermath of this ordeal, our family has been drawn to a mission of raising awareness about drowning prevention and the power of prayer. Inspired by Max's miraculous survival and his divine encounter, we are working on initiatives to teach water safety to children and to share our testimony to encourage others in their faith. We are also exploring the idea of creating a children's book series, drawing from our experience to spread hope and the message of God's protective love.

Through this journey, we have seen the profound impact of community, the strength derived from faith, and the transformative power of a miracle. Max's story is not just about survival; it's a testimony to the presence of Jesus in our moments of deepest need, a reminder of His healing and protective power.

Our family's experience has shown us that miracles do happen, and sometimes, they come to us in the most unexpected ways, teaching us lessons of faith, hope, and love. We have been given a second chance with Max, a miracle that we do not take for granted. Our hearts are filled with gratitude toward the medical staff, our community, and above all, to God, for answering our prayers in a most extraordinary way.

As we move forward, we hold onto the promise that no matter what trials we may face, we are never alone. The power of prayer, the love of our community, and the presence of God in our lives are sources of strength and hope that can overcome any obstacle. Our mission now is to share this hope with the world, to testify to the miracles that can happen when faith, love, and community come together in the name of healing and recovery.

This is not just Max's story; it's a story for anyone who needs to be reminded of the presence of God in their lives, of the protective embrace that surrounds us even in our darkest moments. It's a call to hold onto faith, to believe in miracles, and to never underestimate the power of prayer.

FURTHER REFLECTION

Courtney McKee's story of her son Max's miraculous survival is a profound reminder of the power of faith, prayer, and divine intervention. This testimony invites us to reflect on how we respond to crises and challenges in our lives. It encourages us to trust in God's presence, even when circumstances seem dire. Consider how you have experienced God's protection and provision in your life. Reflect on the moments when prayer brought comfort, guidance, or a miracle in times of need.

Imagine yourself in Courtney's place, witnessing a miracle that defies human understanding. How can you strengthen your faith and deepen your reliance on God's presence in your everyday life? What steps can you take to cultivate a prayerful and trusting heart?

PRAYER

Dear Heavenly Father,

Thank you for the miraculous story of Max and the unwavering faith of his family. Help me to trust in Your presence and to believe in the power of prayer, especially during difficult times. Strengthen my faith and remind me that You are always with me, guiding and protecting me through every challenge. Grant me the courage to rely on Your love and to seek Your presence in all aspects of my life. May my heart be filled with gratitude and hope, knowing that You are always near. Use my experiences to encourage and support others, sharing the message of Your miraculous power and unwavering love.

Amen.

CHAPTER 8
AN AGNOSTIC ENGINEER IS LED TO JESUS AND A NEW CALLING

"Very truly I tell you, whoever hears my word and believes him who sent me has eternal life and will not be judged but has crossed over from death to life."
- John 5:24 (NIV)

Skeptic John's life was forever impacted by a gift. As his father was hospitalized and dying with cancer, a friend gifted a book about near-death experiences (NDEs). As he kept vigil at his father's bedside, John read the entire book. His curiosity was sparked. A thorough investigation of many religious texts and exploration of the evidence led him to know the truth of the Bible and Jesus Christ as his personal Savior. John left his career in engineering for ministry. He is the founder of Gateway Church in Austin, Texas, and the president of Gateway Leadership Initiative, a non-profit organization working to help church-planting pastors and ordinary Christians raise the church out of the culture. He has authored several books including The New York Times best-seller Imagine Heaven (22 languages) and Imagine the God of Heaven. His books expertly detail how many of these reports tie directly to scripture. He also provides critical interpretive keys in discernment with these testimonies. His work has impacted me personally and people around the globe. I believe God has given him a unique and important calling. - Julie

I am **John Burke**, and 45 years ago, I was an agnostic. I've always had a very analytical mind. I constantly questioned how things work and sought to understand them. This mindset extended to questions about the existence of God and Jesus. I figured people probably just deified good people like Jesus over time.

During this period, my dad was dying of cancer, and someone gave him a book that discussed near-death experiences (NDEs). These are instances where people clinically die but are resuscitated by modern medicine or a miracle from God, and they come back talking about experiences of the afterlife. Reading about these experiences, especially the recurring themes of encountering a loving God of brilliant light, and seeing Jesus, made me pause. I thought, *What if this God and Jesus stuff is real?* This sparked my search for truth.

Several years later, I came to faith in Christ through studying the Bible. Eventually, I left engineering and went into ministry. Despite this, my fascination with NDEs continued. Over the years, I kept encountering people who had experienced NDEs. Just this week, I talked to a guy trimming my trees who had one, as did his boss. These encounters kept happening, drawing me deeper into the subject.

Over the last 35 years, I've not only gone to seminary and studied the Bible, but I started a church for skeptics just like me. I've studied over a thousand NDEs and how they tie to the scriptures. I wrote *Imagine Heaven* to showcase the amazing commonalities in these experiences reported by people worldwide—children, doctors, bank presidents, commercial airline pilots, CEOs—saying the same things as people from different cultures. For me, these accounts serve as modern-day evidence that God and heaven are real, echoing what's been said by the Jewish prophets and Jesus.

In recording these reports, it is important to remember that theology is to be based on the Word of God. While experiencers are eyewitnesses of something, they may have a different interpretation of what they saw. For this reason it is very important to have a solid knowledge of scripture as we navigate these testimonies. For instance, if I could travel back to the day of Jesus and interview various witnesses who saw Jesus do miracles, some would say He is the Messiah and some would say He is a sorcerer. They saw the same Jesus, and the same event, but had different interpretations. For this reason we must interpret these in light of what God is saying through the scriptures.

In *Imagine Heaven*, I documented over a hundred NDEs. There are 42 common descriptors of heaven and hell that people have reported, aligning closely with biblical descriptions. The Bible's teachings on the afterlife can often be fragmented, but I believe these NDEs help give color to the Bible's systematic and hopeful picture of what is to come.

Gallup found that one in 25 Americans has had an NDE, and the European Academy of Neuroscience reported one in ten had an NDE across 35 countries. These experiences are not uncommon, though people are often hesitant to share them. Common elements include a heightened sense of reality, leaving the body, traveling through a tunnel or pathway of light, vivid colors beyond what we see here, a life review, and encountering loved ones and a God of light and love.

People who report these testimonies often struggle with words to adequately describe the experience. A common analogy I use is imagining our current life as being lived on a flat, black-and-white painting. Death is like being torn from that painting and experiencing a three-dimensional world of color for the first time. People are grasping to describe this new reality using their limited earthly senses and language.

Many NDEs involve seeing what's happening around them during resuscitation, which often can be verified, convincing many doctors and scientists of their authenticity. For example, Vicki, a blind woman from birth, described details she couldn't have known otherwise. She leaves her body after a car accident. She reports seeing the scene in the operating room and realizing she died. She flies out of the hospital to see a cityscape, travels through a tunnel, and to a heavenly place where light and love emanate from everything. She describes meeting Jesus and being completely captivated. Jesus gives her a life review. In this review she sees two friends who had passed that she knew as children who were also previously blind and handicapped. For the first time, she was able to see their handicaps in this life review. After she was revived, the observations she noted about the young girls and their physical handicaps were later verified by the housemother who had cared for the girls.

A life review in the presence of God is a very common report I hear from experiencers. Interestingly, most say they felt no judgment as they watched their lives replay (see Romans 8:1). Not only do they claim to see their lives, they say that they feel the good and the bad from their own perspective, and from the perspective of others impacted by their actions. I believe this is just what Jesus said that nothing will be hidden, that every motive, thought and deed will be laid bare (Mark 4:22). Paul also said that God wishes to reward us for our good deeds (1 Corinthians 4:5). Most return saying, "God wasn't condemning me, I was condemning myself (see Matthew 12:37). God was trying to love me and support me and help me learn." The number-one thing they learn from this review is that God is love and how we treat one another really matters to God (Mark 12:30-31).

One of the things that helped convince me of these reports' validity are the countless evidential reports of people traveling outside their bodies. There was a woman in London in a hospital who died while giving birth. After she was resuscitated she reported traveling to this amazing place and meeting a God of love and light. She noted that as she came back into the room and floated past the ceiling fan that she noticed a red sticker on the ceiling side of the fan. She convinced a nurse to use a ladder to inspect the top side of the fan blades and there was, just as she described, a red sticker on the ceiling side of the fan.

Another frequent element is meeting a man of light, often identified as Jesus, who emanates a palpable light and love. Jesus' presence is described as more real and brighter than the sun, yet not hard to look at, offering a sense of profound peace and understanding. Never in history, until now, have we been able to hear from so many people across the globe who have been brought back from clinical death…and they are encountering the same captivating God of the Bible.

Some of the powerful revelations that people have in their experience include the power of prayer. Many experiencers have reported seeing the prayers going up to heaven. Descriptions include shooting stars, crystalline streams of light, even contrails shooting up to God the Father. Some have seen angels being dispatched. Some were told that every prayer is recorded in heaven. Many return with a newfound appreciation of the power and importance of prayer.

About 23 percent of NDEs report hellish experiences. These accounts also align with biblical descriptions of hell. The good news is that many people experiencing these hellish NDEs cry out to Jesus to receive forgiveness, and He rescues them, changing their lives profoundly upon return. An important thing to understand is that through the sacrifice and resurrection of Jesus, God has removed every barrier between us and God except one. Our pride and refusal to accept Jesus is the only barrier that can keep us from God. Even in these hellish experiences, many cry out to God for rescue and they are given a second chance. They return completely transformed and often give their lives to ministry.

If you are skeptical, I encourage you to read *Imagine Heaven*, or *Imagine the God of Heaven*, and explore these testimonies. While NDEs sparked my curiosity around the possibility of an afterlife, I came to faith through the historical evidence of Jesus, such as the prophecies in the book of Isaiah, written long before Jesus was born, and which accurately foretold His life and mission. We now have the Dead Sea scrolls. There truly is so much evidence.

I am convinced that NDEs are God's gift to the world-evidence of God's great love for all people. Of all of the wonders of heaven, the beauty, the reunions, the mystery, consistently they would say, "All I wanted to do was be with Him. There's nothing like the presence of the Lord. He is the love we've always wanted."

Jesus said that all the sorrows and sufferings on Earth come from being separated from God. On His last day with the disciples He told them, "I have told you this so that my joy may be in you and your joy may be complete" (John 15:11.) Joy is our birthright. Even in our struggles, when we walk with Jesus, we can experience His joy.

I hope my work can break the box that we often put God in. He is far more majestic, sovereign, loving and in control than we can possibly imagine. But He is also more relatable and fun. He is the God of joy. The Bible at its core is the greatest love story of all time. I pray that all may come to know the profound love and light of God, as revealed through these experiences and the teachings of Jesus.

If you're seeking a connection with Jesus, it begins with a simple, heartfelt prayer. God knows your heart and wants to welcome you. Just express your desire for forgiveness and a relationship with Him, and He will respond.

FURTHER REFLECTION

John Burke's journey from agnosticism to a profound faith illustrates the transformative power of seeking truth and encountering God's love. His fascination with near-death experiences (NDEs) highlights the consistency of these testimonies with biblical descriptions of heaven and the love of Jesus. Reflect on your own questions and doubts about faith and consider how you can seek a deeper understanding of God's presence in your life. How do you respond to evidence of God's love and the testimonies of those who have experienced divine encounters?

Imagine yourself standing before Jesus, experiencing His profound love and peace. How can you allow this vision to deepen your faith and guide your actions? What steps can you take to strengthen your relationship with God and share His love with others?

PRAYER

Dear Heavenly Father,

Thank You for the inspiring journey of John Burke and the profound truths revealed through near-death experiences. Help me to seek a deeper understanding of Your presence and to trust in the evidence of Your love and grace. Strengthen my faith and open my heart to the transformative power of Your love. Guide me in my daily walk with You, and help me to share the hope and joy of knowing You with others. May my life reflect Your light and love, and may I be a beacon of faith and encouragement to those around me.

Amen.

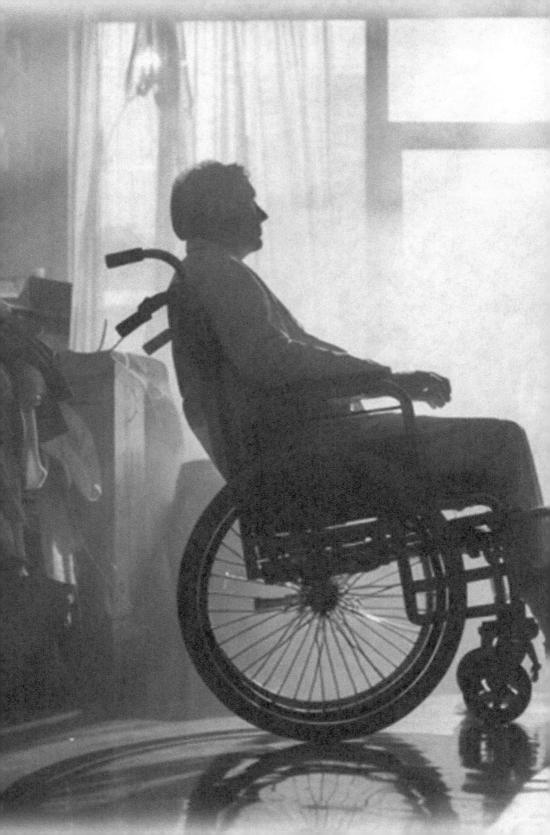

CHAPTER 9
A TEN-YEAR PARALYSIS IS SUPERNATURALLY HEALED!

"I can do all things through Christ who strengthens me."
- Philippians 4:13 (NKJV)

Bryan was enjoying the prime of his life. He was advancing in his law enforcement career, serving and protecting his community when life took a horrific turn. The hand of God is so evident through the love and faith of a committed wife, through a young woman's vision, and a divinely orchestrated moment of the supernatural! Bryan and Meg, thank you for allowing me to share this personal journey! - Julie

I'm **Bryan LaPooh**, a police officer out of New Jersey, and I've got a story that's pretty hard to believe, but it's all true. It all started with a call to check out an icy patch on a road, something pretty routine in my line of work. Only, this time, it was anything but routine. I ended up slipping, and the next thing I knew, I was waking up with doctors forcing a breathing tube down my throat to intubate me as I had broken my neck at C4 and C5 vertebrae. That fall didn't just knock me out; it left the right side of my body completely paralyzed. Surgery did not reverse the paralysis as we had hoped.

The injury was debilitating physically and emotionally. The injury left me with severe headaches. I couldn't swallow. My mobility was severely limited. The simple act of being able to walk was something I had taken for granted. As I fought to recover that first year, I began to have spasticity in the left side. The doctors told me I could be losing the function of the side of my body that was working, which would have meant full paralysis. Roughly four years into this fight, my neck broke again after a nighttime fall as I was reaching for my crutch and my head hit the door hinge. After five years of fighting, the doctors believed there was no chance that my condition would improve. I felt absolutely hopeless.

For over ten years, that was my reality. I went from being this active guy, always on the move, to being stuck in a wheelchair, and then hobbling around with a brace. I couldn't raise my right arm, and my right hand was left permanently curled and stuck (contracted), useless. I was newly married with a baby on the way and was forced to give up my career. Each morning I would slide to the edge of the bed with my left leg and place a brace over my right leg which was the only way I could stand. I saw every doctor you could think of, did all the therapies, often daily, but nothing really changed. I was in pain all the time, not just physically, but deep down, you know? It's like my whole identity was stripped away in an instant.

My journey wasn't just about the physical challenges; the emotional and spiritual battles hit just as hard. When this injury happened, my wife was pregnant and I was doing well in my work. I was advancing and in my prime. The physical battle was constant, the pain and spasticity unrelenting. The migraines were intense and debilitating. The pain was excruciating and never-ending. I found myself wrestling with anger toward God, questioning why this had to happen to me. There were times I told the Lord, "If this is what the rest of life is going to be like, I don't want to be here anymore."

Amid this turmoil, my family, especially my wife Meg, stood by me, offering unwavering support that I struggled to fully appreciate due to my pain. Meg believed God would work a miracle. I became a Christian when

I was 13. I had not witnessed huge miracles. When I was at my lowest point, Meg was strong. When I didn't want to go to church, when I didn't want prayer, Meg was there with faith for the both of us. God blessed me through her persistence and love.

The turning point came in an unexpected way, thanks to Meg's perseverance. She convinced me to attend a prayer conference, presenting it as a combined gift for her birthday, Mother's Day, and Christmas. She had an overwhelming conviction and expectancy that the time for my healing was now. I remember hearing conflicting voices in my head with the decision over this event. One message in my head, "Why go? Nothing is going to change. You are paralyzed for life. You know what the doctors said." Yet another voice was saying, "Take it." I didn't understand what, "Take it" meant. Meg's relentless faith and her tireless fight for my healing shone brightly, even when things looked bleak. Her belief in prayer and divine intervention was a constant source of hope and strength for us both, showcasing her as a true warrior of faith.

The first day we arrived at the conference, I didn't expect much; I mean, after ten years, you kind of wrestle with hopelessness. But something happened that night. I can't fully explain it, but I felt the power of the Holy Spirit and I felt my faith coming back. On the second day of the event, I felt more of the pain, lies, and trauma being lifted. That evening when we broke for dinner, I told Meg, "I think I am going to take my brace off tonight." Meg was thrilled to hear this.

At the end of that night, the leaders began calling up specific conditions for healing. One after another, everything imaginable was called except for my paralysis. For a moment I felt that once again God was passing me by. Finally, we are in the closing minutes of the conference when the speaker offers, "If there is anyone with any other ailment that needs prayer, please come forward and our student prayer team will pray for you." At that moment, I felt a pull on my neck and a voice, "Get up," urging me to go forward. At that moment, despite all my years of skepticism and hurt, I listened and, with the help of my brace, went directly to the altar. Once at the front, the same force and voice directed me to, "turn left," toward a young girl on the prayer team.

She asked, "What do you need prayer for?" I explained I had a spinal cord injury. She placed her hand on my chest. I explained, "I need you to put your hand on my neck." As she laid her hand on my neck, the spot where my life had changed forever, a warmth enveloped me, unlike anything I'd ever felt. The lights went out at that moment. I was assisted to the ground and the only thing I can remember is colors flashing in front of my eyes. It was very surreal and difficult to put into words. Eventually, I came back to a state of awareness.

The young woman asked me, "How do you feel?" I answered, "I feel tremendous peace and warmth." She asked, "Can you do anything that you couldn't do before the prayer?" I looked at my right clenched hand and I willed my hand to move. My fingers started to wiggle. Then I began to start squeezing my right hand. My right hand straightened out! When I saw this, a huge peace came over me. This had never happened in over ten years of prayer. I was in awe. I thought, if my hand is moving, then my leg has got to move as well. I scoot myself to the altar and attempt to sit up and remove the brace from my leg.

One of the praying students says, "Are you sure you want to do that?" I replied, "Oh yeah, I am sure." I threw the brace to the side and I asked for some help getting upright. Three people helped me to get up and continued praying for me as I began to move. They helped support me as I started to try to take small steps forward. As we continued to pray and take steps, my leg got stronger. Suddenly they are now only supporting me by holding my hand. Now the brace that once kept me upright is on the floor near the altar.

Meg always said the day I got healed that she would run up and down the streets shouting with joy. I got healed so late at night, near midnight. The church was nearly empty. We walked out of the church that night in shock, saying absolutely nothing, almost numb and unable to process the miracle that had just taken place. Meg and I needed time to absorb the undeniable miracle that had occurred.

The next day I returned to thank the young woman who prayed over me. She shared something that left me absolutely stunned. She told me that two months before, she had a vision where she was praying for a man with a paralyzed and contracted hand. The hand God showed her was my hand. Hearing her share this, knowing she had seen this moment long before it happened, it felt like a divine appointment had been set for me, and I had walked right into it.

As I followed up with the young lady there was another gentleman present. He explained that he was standing behind me just before I was assisted to the floor when she touched my neck. He was approaching the prayer team to receive prayer for his shoulder injury. As he reflexively went to brace me as I was falling, his hands touched my back and his shoulder was instantly healed.

I found myself still reaching for my crutch and brace for the next month and a half simply out of habit. Going back to see the doctors was interesting, to say the least. They were just as floored as I was. Here I was, walking into their office, doing things they had all but written off as impossible for me. My file, thick with years of treatments, therapies, and grim prognoses, didn't match the man standing before them. They poured over my reports, trying to find a medical explanation for my recovery. But deep down, I knew, and they suspected, that what had happened transcended the bounds of medical science. It was a miracle from God.

As I reflect back, I see how God was clearly with me and working in my life. I couldn't see it because the enemy was working so hard in my thoughts telling me lies. God was not merely walking with me, He was carrying me. The brace, just one example of a blessing, was so new and advanced and really was such a gift from God until I received the needed healing. I realize how many blessings and things that I took for granted. I make an effort now to stop each day and thank God for the blessings, the ones I notice and ones I may not perceive.

So here I am, sharing my story with you. I'm not just a cop from New Jersey who got lucky; I'm a living, breathing example of what God can do. My whole life, my very existence, has taken on a new meaning. Everything I thought I knew about faith, hope, and the possibility of miracles has been turned on its head. If you're out there struggling, feeling like you're at the end of your rope, I want you to hear this: there is hope. Instead of running away from God in those moments, get even closer to Him. It is hard and I am not going to say that it is easy. I've walked through the darkest valleys, battled the deepest despair, and I've come out on the other side. It didn't happen overnight, but it happened. And if it can happen to me, it can happen to you too. So keep PRAYING, and stay open to the possibility that your miracle is just around the corner.

FURTHER REFLECTION

Bryan LaPooh's testimony of healing from paralysis is a powerful reminder of God's ability to perform miracles and the importance of unwavering faith. His journey from despair to miraculous recovery challenges us to trust in God's timing and never lose hope, even in the darkest moments. Reflect on the areas in your life where you feel hopeless or burdened, and consider how deepening your faith and relying on God can bring transformation.

Imagine yourself in Bryan's place, experiencing a miraculous healing after years of suffering. How can you cultivate a similar trust in God's plan for your life? What steps can you take to strengthen your faith and remain open to the possibility of miracles?

PRAYER

Dear Heavenly Father,

Thank You for Bryan LaPooh's inspiring testimony of healing and renewed faith. Help me to trust in Your power and timing, especially during times of struggle and despair. Strengthen my faith and remind me that Your love and miracles are always possible. Guide me to lean on You in every aspect of my life and to remain open to the blessings and healing You have in store for me. May my life be a testament to Your grace and power, bringing hope and encouragement to those around me.

Amen.

CHAPTER 10
MY SON SURVIVED A PLANE CRASH

"The angel of the Lord encamps around those who fear him, and he delivers them."
- Psalm 34:7 (NIV)

Seven-year-old Mason miraculously survived a plane crash. His mother Lindsay shares how God moved through prayer, people and angels to protect and heal her son. - Julie

I am **Lindsay Jeter**. My son was the only survivor of a plane crash. I had no idea that my son, Mason, was going flying. It was his dad's weekend with him. They were supposed to spend the weekend together, as they did every other weekend. I was busy cleaning out my classroom for the summer after church, completely unaware of the impending disaster. Suddenly, cops arrived at my home and told me that there had been an accident. They didn't give me many details at first. They just said that Mason had been involved in a plane crash and that I needed to go to the hospital immediately. On the way to the hospital, I kept asking the policeman if Mason was going to be okay. All he could tell me was that

Mason was stable for now, but he didn't have any more information. The uncertainty and fear during that drive were almost unbearable.

When I arrived at the hospital, I finally saw Mason, but he was unrecognizable. His face was swollen, and he had multiple fractures and injuries all over his body. He had a broken nose, multiple facial fractures, a broken right femur, a large laceration on his leg, liver laceration, lung contusions, brain contusions, and a broken left foot. He had also suffered a chemical burn on his leg. He was in a medically induced coma to manage the trauma his body had undergone. Seeing him in that state was devastating. The loss of life in the crash simultaneously was also devastating. We prayed for all affected by this loss as we prayed for Mason.

The doctors were initially uncertain about his recovery. Mason's condition was critical, and his numbers, particularly his kidney function, started to fail. They prepared to transfer him to a specialist in New Orleans due to the impending storm, but after a night of intense prayer and coordination between doctors via technology, his numbers miraculously began to improve the next morning. I firmly believe that this turnaround was due to the power of prayer.

Despite the severity of his injuries, there were clear signs that divine intervention played a role in Mason's survival. The details of the crash were almost unbelievable. Mason's father died on impact, but Mason's seat belt broke, causing him to be ejected from the plane. He flew through a narrow space between two trees and landed on a soft pallet of leaves and pine straw. This prevented him from seeing the horrific scene inside the plane and minimized his injuries. My uncle, an experienced pilot, later confirmed that the space between those trees was so narrow that it was a miracle Mason didn't hit either of them.

When Mason was found, he was in severe pain and crying out for his father. The EMTs and paramedics had to sedate him to transport him safely. The forestry department had to clear a path for the ambulance, which underscores the complexity and difficulty of the rescue operation. It was truly a team effort to save Mason's life, and I am forever grateful to everyone involved.

Throughout this ordeal, my faith was profoundly strengthened. On the way to the hospital, a peace came over me after I began praying out loud.

It was an indescribable sense of calm that reassured me that Mason would survive, although I had no idea what his recovery would look like. This peace stayed with me, guiding me through the difficult days ahead.

One of the most striking aspects of this experience was the support from my community and the many instances of what I believe were divine signs. For example, a close friend of mine, while grocery shopping, felt an overwhelming presence of angels around her at the exact time of the crash. She didn't know what was happening but sensed something significant was unfolding. When she later learned about Mason's accident, she understood that the angels she felt were there to protect him.

During this ordeal, God woke me up one morning and reminded me of the angels I prayed over my children daily. He affirmed that He had dispatched them to protect Mason. I was also led to Psalm 91 and Psalm 34, which talk about angels guarding us. Before the accident, I felt a strong urge to fast and pray for a friend. That day, I sent a song by Casting Crowns called "I Will Praise You in the Storm," not realizing I would soon be living those words.

Telling Mason about his father's death was one of the hardest things I had to do. I prayed for God's help, and miraculously, the trauma physician's assistant, Rachel, arrived just as Mason asked about his dad. Her support during that moment was a divine provision. Mason's recovery was slow and challenging. After ten days, he was extubated and began to show signs of recognition, which was a huge relief. The doctors closely monitored his cognitive functions, and as days passed, he started to show remarkable improvements. By April 2021, he even made it to gifted classes at school, a testament to his mental resilience and recovery. Mason's physical recovery also progressed; he returned to playing baseball and even made the All-Star team the year after his accident, although he still walks with a limp due to his leg injury.

Despite his physical challenges, Mason is a happy and spiritually strong boy. He continues to undergo physical therapy and sees a chiropractor regularly. The emotional healing process is ongoing, and he receives counseling to help him cope with the trauma and loss he experienced. His strength and positivity are truly inspiring, and he has a wonderful support system, including a loving family and a great youth group at church.

Reflecting on the entire experience, I am constantly reminded of the power of faith and prayer. Throughout Mason's ordeal, I saw numerous signs of God's presence and intervention. One particular moment that stands out is when God woke me up one night and reminded me of the angels I had prayed to guard my children every day. He assured me that those angels were real and that they had protected Mason during the crash. This revelation was incredibly comforting and reinforced my belief in the power of prayer and divine protection.

Another significant spiritual experience was related to the Asbury Revival. One night, while reflecting on the revival's 16-day duration, I felt compelled to learn more about it. Discovering that it lasted almost 400 hours, I was struck by the number 400 and its biblical significance. God reminded me that He had been silent for 400 years between the Old and New Testaments, but He is no longer silent. He is awakening our spirits, calling us to recognize His presence and work in our lives.

To anyone facing a crisis, whether it's a financial struggle, a health issue, or another challenging situation, I want to emphasize the importance of faith. In those darkest moments, turning to God and leaning on His strength can provide the comfort and guidance needed to navigate through the storm. God's presence is constant, and He offers us peace and hope, even in the most difficult times. Embrace His word, pray earnestly, and trust that He is with you every step of the way.

In closing, I want to express my deepest gratitude for the prayers and support we received during Mason's recovery. The power of prayer is real, and I am thankful for the many miracles we witnessed. Mason's story is a testament to God's faithfulness and the incredible strength that faith can provide. I hope Mason's journey inspires and encourages others facing their own trials.

FURTHER REFLECTION

Lindsay Jeter's story powerfully illustrates the impact of unwavering faith and the miraculous power of prayer. Mason's survival and recovery from a devastating plane crash highlight the presence of divine intervention and the strength that comes from trusting in God's plan. The experiences of angelic protection and community support emphasize the importance of recognizing and relying on God's guidance, even in the darkest times. Reflect on your own experiences and challenges. Consider how prayer and faith have played roles in your journey. Think about the ways you can deepen your trust in God and remain open to His guidance and intervention. How can you rely more on prayer and faith to navigate future difficulties?

PRAYER

Lord,

We thank You for Your constant presence and the miraculous power of prayer. Help us to trust in Your plan and find comfort in Your protection. Strengthen our faith and guide us through difficult times, reminding us of Your unwavering love and care. May we always turn to You in our darkest moments and find peace and hope in Your word. Use our experiences to inspire and encourage others, and may our lives reflect Your faithfulness and grace.

Amen.

CHAPTER 11
A TWELVE-YEAR-OLD GIRL MEETS JESUS

"Be strong and of good courage, do not fear nor be afraid of them;
for the Lord your God, He is the One who goes with you.
He will not leave you nor forsake you."
- Deuteronomy 31:6 (NKJV)

Susanne shares that her family didn't speak about heaven or Jesus. She meets him for the first time at age twelve when she dies in a tragic accident. Her experience in the heavenly realm is still jumping off the pages of her Bible today! Her physical healing alone was so miraculous the hospital wanted to erect a plaque to commemorate the event. The kindness, warmth and joy of Jesus radiate beautifully from Susanne today and I am so honored to share her miracle! - Julie

I am **Susanne Seymoure**, and I want to share with you a journey that transformed my life, a journey that took me from a tragic accident on a ski slope to an extraordinary encounter with Jesus Christ and a visit to heaven.

My story begins with a backdrop of my family's miraculous survival through the Holocaust. My family's history is marked by heroism and resilience, eventually leading us to migrate to the United States, where we hoped for a new beginning. At the age of 12, my life took a dramatic turn during a skiing trip with my family. It was supposed to be a beautiful day on a private ski slope, a day of joy and family bonding. However, it quickly turned into a nightmare. My scarf got caught in the ski lift cable, and the force broke my neck. The accident was horrific, and I was presumed dead for about 45 minutes.

As I lay in the snow, approaching what seemed like the end, I had an encounter that would forever change my understanding of life, death, and what lies beyond. A man approached me through a blinding light, introducing Himself as Jesus, accompanied by two angels wearing armor. I will never forget those hands that reached out to me. They radiated such love and peace, even information. It was almost overwhelming. He communicated with me, not through words but through a profound sense of love and understanding that transcended human language.

His eyes radiated a golden light, filled with compassion and wisdom. In those moments, He let me know He was my Savior, and I was safe. The eyes of Jesus were captivating. They capture you with love, with a peace that is grand and hard to describe. They had a very distinct glow of gold in them. I could say there were hues of different colors, but the color was secondary to the love you feel coming through them. I didn't want to look away from Him. I get emotional just thinking about looking into His eyes.

Jesus told me He was taking me home. He carried me to heaven, a kingdom organized and filled with beauty beyond comprehension. In heaven, I encountered a council of beings who deliberated on my fate. The feeling of being home was undeniable, yet I knew my family on Earth still needed me. I met Melchizedek, who imparted wisdom and showed me the records of all beings. He was very serious. The knowledge and love I received in heaven was boundless.

Faced with the choice to stay in heaven or return to Earth, my heart was torn. Despite the allure of staying in this place of unconditional love, my thoughts turned to my mother, who had already endured so much loss. I couldn't bear the thought of adding to her pain. This concern for my mother played a crucial role in the council's discussion about my fate. In the end, I chose to return to Earth. There was such care from everyone in heaven. They explained to me that it was not going to be easy and that returning to this life would mean pain. The longer I was there I wanted to stay, but my final decision was to return to my grieving mother.

Just before Jesus took me back, I witnessed something even more extraordinary. I looked over the hills and there were points of light that formed what I can only refer to as a massive golden hand of light. It extended and connected to Jesus and they were one. I was overcome with this awareness of the expanse of this Kingdom. My spirit felt more alive than I can explain in witnessing this light. Immediately, as that light touched me, we returned to the scene and Jesus stayed with me and comforted me until my family arrived. I remember my spirit coming back into my body and suddenly feeling the cold snow. Jesus told me He would always be with me.

As my family arrived they were curious about who I was talking to and shocked to see me very injured but alive. In spite of the trauma, I couldn't contain my excitement for what I had experienced. It was the greatest event of my life. We call it my second birthday. The physical miraculous healing I experienced left the hospital staff in awe. The nuns wanted to erect a plaque to commemorate the undeniable miracle. My neck was healed, and I was alive against all odds.

Returning to Earth was not without its challenges. I struggled to reconcile the divine love and presence I had experienced in heaven with the reality of my physical existence. I sought Jesus in churches, longing to feel His presence as vividly as I did on the day of my accident. My journey led me to understand that the divine love I experienced is not confined to a place or a moment; it is always with us, guiding us through the challenges of life.

Before this incident, I had never read the Bible. As I began to read, it was amazing to see it come to life. It has given me context for so many things that I witnessed and helped me have an even deeper understanding of what I learned. It is so nice to know that we have such great help and love from heaven available to us if we choose it. God wants you to choose Him. If we are forced to love, it isn't truly love.

One of the most profound moments in sharing my story came when I encountered a young man who had also experienced a visit to heaven. His family wheeled him toward me at a book signing, and when our eyes met, I saw the same golden light I had seen in Jesus' eyes. He had been in a coma and had not spoken until that moment. His first words were to me, confirming that he too had met Jesus. He fell into my arms, shared what he experienced, and told me he didn't want to come back. He had been through so much and was still processing the events. Knowing he was not alone gave him comfort. It was a moment I will never forget. This encounter was a powerful affirmation of the reality of heaven and the transformative power of these experiences.

Jesus healed me from this injury but has continued to guide me in life. He led me to a wonderful career in nursing to help bring healing to others. Ultimately He led me to teach nursing. I enjoyed such a blessed time in equipping those with a heart to serve with compassion. He has guided every aspect of my life, and I continue to walk with Him each day.

Jesus wants us to know that He is with us, always ready to welcome us with open arms, regardless of our past or the mistakes we think we've made. His love is unconditional, and He invites us to connect with Him. The closer you draw to Him, the more exciting life becomes. There is so much joy too, it is not about just reaching out to Him when you are down and out. Life is so much richer and more meaningful. Let Him work through you. Don't be afraid, because He will never hurt you.

In sharing my story, I've learned that each of us has a unique journey with God. He meets us where we are, in our moments of doubt, fear, and even in our moments of joy. My encounter with Jesus on the ski slope was just the beginning of a lifelong relationship that has guided me through every step of my life. His promise to never leave me was not just for the moment of my return to this earthly life but for every moment that followed.

FURTHER REFLECTION

Susanne Seymoure's miraculous experience challenges us to reflect on the presence and love of Jesus in our lives. Her journey from a tragic accident to a divine encounter with Jesus highlights the reality of God's love and the promise of His presence. Reflect on your own life and consider the moments when you have felt God's presence or needed His guidance. How can you draw closer to Him and trust in His unconditional love?

Imagine yourself in Susanne's place, experiencing the profound peace and love of Jesus. How can you cultivate a similar awareness of His presence in your daily life? What steps can you take to strengthen your faith and remain open to His guidance and love?

PRAYER

Dear Heavenly Father,

Thank You for Susanne Seymoure's inspiring testimony and the profound love she experienced with Jesus. Help me to recognize Your presence in my life and to trust in Your unwavering love and guidance. Strengthen my faith and open my heart to the transformative power of Your love. Guide me to live each day with the awareness of Your presence, and help me to share Your love and hope with others. May my life reflect Your grace and bring encouragement to those around me.

Amen.

CHAPTER 12
AN ATTORNEY'S JOURNEY TO HEALING FAITH

"Jesus said to him, 'If you can believe, all things are possible to him who believes.'"
- Mark 9:23 (NKJV)

Steve was a young attorney who's life was radically changed when he personally witnessed undeniable supernatural healing miracles. These events sparked his faith and ultimately led him from law to ministry. He has been a pastor at Lakewood Church for over 20 years and has ministered faithfully to thousands of patients and their families for 25 years in the largest medical center in the world-Houston Texas Medical Center. He is also the founder and president of Living Hope Chaplaincy. There aren't many people who I have met that have this man's passion for seeing people get a revelation of God as a healer. His work has been a blessing to me personally! - Julie

I am **Steve Austin**, and if you rewound 30 years ago, you'd find me as probably the least likely person to be speaking about healing. I was a young attorney, established in the rational world of law, where everything hinges on facts and evidence. My background was in denominations that didn't teach anything about healing. It simply wasn't on my radar. I had never experienced any health issues myself, so the concept of miraculous healing was as foreign to me as a country I had never visited.

My journey into the world of healing began unexpectedly. My brother-in-law invited me to a fellowship of Christian businessmen's luncheon, where a short-term missionary shared tales of miraculous healings from his Crusades around the world. I was skeptical, to say the least. Yet, something about his stories intrigued me, and sparked a curiosity that I couldn't shake off. Following the luncheon, I introduced myself to him and, on a whim, expressed my interest in joining one of his mission trips. He was planning a trip to India in a month, and he invited me along. I accepted, partly driven by my skepticism. I wanted to see these alleged miracles for myself.

India was a revelation. We traveled to very remote villages in the Northeast, close to the Burma border. I approached this trip with the mindset of a doubting Thomas. My legal background urged me to seek proof, so I even hired a videographer to document everything we would encounter. I expected to debunk the myths of miraculous healings. Instead, what I experienced shattered every preconception I had about God and His power. The miracles I witnessed were undeniable and transformative. I saw people healed of blindness, deafness, and paralysis right before my eyes, with no theatrics, just the raw power of faith in action.

One particular incident stands out vividly in my memory. I prayed for a man paralyzed on one side of his body due to a stroke. With a simple prayer, invoking the name of Jesus and commanding healing, he began to lift his arm for the first time in who knows how long. As he praised God, his arm rose higher, and his paralysis was cured. Witnessing such a profound transformation firsthand changed the trajectory of my life. I encountered God in a way that was entirely new to me, breaking free from the constraints of my previous beliefs.

My return to the United States was met with introspection. I pondered why such miraculous occurrences seemed so rare in my home country. I questioned God about this, and His response was clear: in America, and other Western countries, we often place our faith more in doctors, medicine, and technology than in God. This isn't to say that medical professionals aren't valuable—God uses them in powerful ways. However, the reliance on human abilities can sometimes overshadow our faith in the divine. This realization prompted a significant shift in my perspective. I began to seek God not just as a last resort but as the first point of call in times of need.

This first trip led to many more, each further embedding me in the ministry of healing. I journeyed to Egypt, witnessing more miracles, and then to Israel, where I experienced baptism in the Holy Spirit—an event that was foreign to even my vocabulary at the time. Each step on this path drew me deeper into a relationship with God, transforming me from a skeptic into a fervent believer in His power to heal and work miracles today.

My evolution from an attorney to a chaplain and a minister of healing wasn't instantaneous. It was a gradual process, marked by significant spiritual milestones and continuous learning. As I grew in my understanding and experience of God's healing power, I also encountered the skepticism and curiosity that had once defined my own approach to faith. I realized that part of my calling was to bridge the gap between disbelief and faith, guiding others to experience the miraculous power of God in their lives.

I started praying for people within my community, witnessing God's healing touch time and again. One of the most memorable moments was praying for a young man with cancer deemed inoperable by some of the best doctors. After prayer, he was completely healed, a testament to the fact that God's power knows no bounds. This journey has taught me the profound truth that while medicine and technology have their place, they are not the ultimate source of healing. God is.

In my ministry, I've learned to fight not just with the tools of this world but with the power of faith. I've learned the importance of what I term "Bulldog Faith"—a persistent, tenacious faith that refuses to let go of God's promises. I've seen the power of creating a "faith cocoon," a space where belief in God's power to heal is nurtured and protected from doubt and negativity. This journey has been about more than just witnessing miracles; it's been about learning to participate in the work God is doing in the world, through prayer, faith, and action.

Through years of experience, study, and witnessing miracles I have become passionate about helping others receive their breakthrough in the area of healing. My heart is to equip others, helping them understand that God's will is always for healing, that there is power in their words, and there is a more effective way to pray using scripture. God loves it when we pray His Word back to Him. I also think it is important to understand that God wants us healed completely. If there are times we are not seeing a physical healing, He may be working to heal something in our soul. Understanding that there could be barriers blocking us from healing: unforgiveness, resentment, disappointment, spiritual issues. It is a battle that is worth fighting.

To anyone listening, I want to say this: God loves you immensely. He hasn't forgotten about you, and He's more than capable of working miracles in your life. No matter the battle you're facing, keep your faith strong, persist in prayer, and stay open to the miraculous ways God wants to move in your life. Remember, with God, all things are possible.

FURTHER REFLECTION

Steve Austin's journey from skepticism to faith highlights the transformative power of witnessing God's miracles firsthand. His experience teaches us the importance of placing our faith in God above all else, even in a world reliant on technology and medicine. Reflect on your own beliefs and the areas where you might be relying more on human solutions than on God's power. How can you cultivate a deeper faith that seeks God first in every situation?

Imagine yourself in Steve's position, witnessing miraculous healings that defy human explanation. How can you nurture a "bulldog faith" that holds steadfast to God's promises? What steps can you take to create a "faith cocoon," protecting and nurturing your belief in God's healing power?

PRAYER

Dear Heavenly Father,

Thank You for Steve Austin's inspiring journey from skepticism to faith and the miraculous healings he witnessed. Help me to trust in Your power and seek You first in all situations. Strengthen my faith and remind me that with You, all things are possible. Guide me to rely on Your promises and to persist in prayer, believing in Your ability to bring healing and transformation. May my life be a testament to Your love and power, and may I share Your hope and healing with those around me.

Amen.

CHAPTER 13
COMBATTING DARKNESS WITH DELIVERANCE MINISTRY

"Behold, I give you the authority to trample on serpents and scorpions, and over all the power of the enemy, and nothing shall by any means hurt you."
- Luke 10:19 (NKJV)

Percy was a young Presbyterian pastor with 7 years of theology training when he was introduced to the ministry of deliverance at a Derek Prince event. He and his young wife Sara Jo's first church was in New Orleans, a city permeated by spiritual darkness. The Lord would use their experiences there as a launching pad for a powerful deliverance ministry. For over 50 years they have helped countless individuals find spiritual freedom. Percy is a seminary chaplain and is on the leadership team of Charlotte Leadership Forum. He is the founder of Glorious Freedom Ministries based in Charlotte. He and Sara Jo have collaborated with psychiatrists and respected leaders. I am grateful to have learned about this topic from Percy and Sara Jo as I have received countless testimonies involving deliverance from the demonic. I have been blessed personally by their ministry. Breaking free of spiritual oppression is a miracle! - Julie

I am **Percy Burns**, and I find immense joy in sharing my journey and insights into the profound and often misunderstood realm of deliverance ministry. My experiences, deeply rooted in biblical scripture and personal encounters with the spiritual realm, have shaped a life dedicated to understanding and combating the forces of darkness through the power and authority of Jesus Christ.

My personal path to embracing deliverance ministry was unconventional. After completing my seminary education, I found myself in New Orleans, a city with a palpable presence of spiritual darkness. We were minutes from the French Quarter, an area where there was a regular practice of voodoo and witchcraft.

God began preparing us for ministry during our time in New Orleans. I was working in the yard one day when a woman approached me. She shared that her car had broken down and she needed to use our phone. I led her to our front door and explained this to my wife, who was inside with our 2-month-old baby boy. As soon as she stepped over the threshold of our home, she fell straight to the ground and began slithering across the floor like a snake. We were looking at her in astonishment. We didn't want her to get near our baby, so we began rebuking in the name of Jesus whatever it was that possessed this woman, and crying out to the Lord to protect our precious infant. We knew very little about spiritual warfare at this time in our lives.

Suddenly, she stopped slithering and crawled up on the sofa as if nothing had happened. I asked her if she had any idea what she had just done. I tried to talk to her about Jesus, but she didn't want to hear a word. She told us that she was a member of a cult just down the street from our home. She made her call and left. This incident really opened our eyes to the reality of the demonic. The Lord clearly revealed to us that He is our protection. The presence the woman encountered when she crossed the threshold of our home was the Holy Spirit. It knocked her to the floor.

Hungering for more of the presence of Jesus, I was led to attend a three-day seminar taught by distinguished former Cambridge professor Derek Prince. It was here, influenced by his teaching, that I was introduced to the reality of spiritual warfare and deliverance. This experience reshaped my understanding and approach to ministry, leading me to recognize the widespread need for deliverance, even among believers.

The topic of discussion on the second night of the seminar was spiritual warfare. Here I sat, a young Presbyterian pastor, with four years of Bible college and three years of seminary training hearing about demonic possession for the first time. I was such a straight-laced pastor, I wouldn't allow the organist to play soft music during the offering as not to emotionally manipulate the congregation, and here I am in the middle of a deliverance situation with 500 people. After an hour of teaching, the speaker gave an invitation for guests to come forward for ministry. Roughly one-third of the room went forward. My eyes were wide as I took in everything I could on deliverance.

Derek Prince was very matter-of-fact and biblical. Given the large number of people coming forward, He begins to start calling out spirits from the group. This is called group deliverance. Near the end of the evening, my wife and I were walking to the car. All of a sudden, something started happening to me. My wife was unsure what to make of this, perhaps she felt I was about to get sick, so she suggested we go back inside. Someone with the ministry met us and I believe their prayer casted, demonic spirits out of me. It was brief, to the point, and effective. In no way was I embarrassed.

The third night of the conference was about the fullness of the Holy Spirit. I believe that when a person becomes a believer the Holy Spirit comes to dwell in him, but I also believe the Holy Spirit can come in greater measure. In the days that followed I honestly felt a change. I felt a freedom. Life was better. Those last two nights of the conference were absolutely life-changing for us and have influenced the last 50 years of our ministry.

Impressed with this newfound freedom and understanding of the biblical teaching of deliverance, my wife and I were excited about the potential to help others who were in spiritual bondage. I began to minister to others. People were seeing their anxiety, fears, suicidal tendencies, and various issues resolved, marriages and relationships being healed. Some were telling us that it was life-changing.

Delving into the basics, it's essential to clarify the concepts of demons, spiritual warfare, and deliverance. Demons, also known as evil spirits or unclean spirits, are fallen angels cast out from God's presence due to their rebellion. These spiritual beings, led by Satan, seek to fulfill the work of darkness, influencing and tormenting individuals. Deliverance, therefore, is the process of casting these spirits out, liberating individuals from their grasp through the authority granted to us by Jesus Christ. While a Christian cannot be possessed by the devil, they can be oppressed.

My love for the biblical narrative and the miraculous events surrounding Jesus' birth has taken me to Israel 17 times. These journeys have not only strengthened my faith but have also provided me with a tangible connection to the stories that form the bedrock of our Christian beliefs. The reality of spiritual beings, both angelic and demonic, is vividly present in the biblical account, reminding us of the ongoing spiritual battle that affects our physical world.

Jesus Christ's role in deliverance marks a significant shift from the Old Testament, where deliverance was not a prominent theme. With His arrival, casting out demons became a central aspect of His ministry, highlighting the arrival of the kingdom of God through such miraculous acts. Jesus' confrontations with demonic forces underscored His authority over them, setting a precedent for the church to follow in His footsteps. As the Bible states clearly, He is the same yesterday, today, and forever.

Recognizing signs of demonic influence can be challenging, as they often manifest in ways that mimic psychological or emotional issues. However, persistent thoughts of destruction, uncontrollable behaviors, or profound fears can indicate demonic oppression. It's crucial to discern these signs carefully, always seeking the guidance of the Holy Spirit and the wisdom of Scripture. Discernment is needed to differentiate between mental illness and demonic oppression. For this reason, I have been invited to collaborate with psychiatrists on occasion.

Demons can gain access to individuals through various means, including generational curses, traumatic experiences, sinful behaviors, multiple intimate partners, illicit drugs, and engagement with the occult. Understanding these access points is essential for effective ministry, as it allows us to address not only the symptoms but also the root causes of spiritual bondage.

The process of deliverance involves casting out demons and ensuring the individual is filled with the Holy Spirit to prevent any spiritual vacuum that could invite further demonic influence. This aspect of ministry underscores the necessity of holistic spiritual care, emphasizing the importance of ongoing spiritual growth and protection. For example, if you are commanding a spirit of anxiety to go, you want to call in the opposite spirit of peace. This avoids the vacuum.

In my ministry, I've observed that deliverance rarely conforms to the sensational portrayals seen in popular media. More often, it's a quiet, gentle process marked by profound peace and liberation. This discrepancy highlights the need for a grounded, biblical approach to deliverance, one that focuses on the authority of Christ rather than the theatrics of confrontation.

That being said, I have seen the dramatic. A respected psychiatrist brought a client to me for deliverance. He was a young strong man. As I was ministering deliverance over him he reached down and broke the solid wood arms off of my chair like they were toothpicks. He started screaming at me, "I'll kill you, I'll kill you!" Luckily, we came out of that without incident. At times you see a second pair of eyes, some hysterical laughter, or emotion, even coughing or spitting. There have definitely been some dramatic moments, but for the most part, it is a straightforward time of prayer with the Holy Spirit leading.

Ministering to children and conducting spiritual housecleanings are also vital components of deliverance ministry. Both practices underscore the pervasive nature of spiritual warfare and the need for vigilance in protecting our homes and loved ones from demonic influences. Parents need to be involved in the deliverance of their children.

Despite historical resistance within the church, I've witnessed a growing acceptance of deliverance ministry. This shift, supported by collaboration with medical professionals who acknowledge the spiritual dimensions of healing, suggests a broader recognition of the comprehensive nature of Christ's ministry.

For those seeking to delve deeper into this ministry, the Bible remains the foundational resource, supplemented by numerous books and teachings that explore the nuances of spiritual warfare and deliverance.

Engaging with these materials can provide valuable insights and equip believers with the tools needed to effectively combat the forces of darkness.

My prayer is for the liberation and healing of all who encounter the forces of darkness. Through the authority of Jesus Christ, we have the power to overcome and to bring His light into the darkest of places. May we all embrace this call with courage, faith, and a deep love for those we serve.

FURTHER REFLECTION

Percy Burns' journey into deliverance ministry reveals the importance of understanding and confronting spiritual warfare through the authority of Jesus Christ. His experiences highlight the reality of demonic influences and the power of faith in overcoming them. Reflect on your own life and consider areas where you may feel spiritually oppressed or in need of deliverance. How can you strengthen your faith and seek God's protection against these forces?

Imagine yourself standing before Jesus, seeking His guidance and protection against spiritual darkness. How can you cultivate a deeper reliance on His power and authority in your daily life? What steps can you take to engage in spiritual warfare with confidence and trust in God's victory?

PRAYER

Dear Heavenly Father,

Thank You for Percy Burns' testimony and the insights into the realm of deliverance ministry. Help me to recognize the reality of spiritual warfare and to trust in Your authority and power to overcome it. Strengthen my faith and guide me to seek Your protection and deliverance in all areas of my life. Grant me the wisdom to discern spiritual influences and the courage to confront them with the authority of Jesus Christ. May my life be a testament to Your victory over darkness, bringing light and hope to those around me.

Amen.

CHAPTER 14

WITNESSING HEAVENLY MIRACLES FROM A PASTOR'S PERSPECTIVE (RESURRECTION MIRACLE)

"You are the God who does wonders;
You have declared Your strength among the peoples."
- Psalm 77:14 (NKJV)

Pastor Matt admits the last few years of ministry post-pandemic have been exhausting. A committed leader at Sandals Church in California, he prayed fervently for the Holy Spirit to lead him to a path forward. He heard a clear word from Jesus-HEALER. Stepping out in faith, he was obedient in speaking and teaching on healing. He was astonished by what God did in his church. I loved hearing what God led him to write in his book about healing miracles and how we anchor our faith when the answer to our prayers may not be in the desired timing or response. I respect pastor Matt's humility and transparency. An excellent resource that focuses first on the Healer! - Julie

I am **Matt Brown**, and my life's journey has been one marked by a series of astonishing encounters that I can only describe as miraculous. Growing up in a Baptist community, my introduction to the concept of miracles came later in life. This delayed introduction did not deter my fascination but rather fueled my desire to understand and share these profound experiences. My story, encapsulated in the pages of a book I was compelled to write, is a testament to the power of God's intervention in our lives—often in ways we least expect but most need.

My personal testimony begins with my upbringing, grounded in strong Baptist traditions where the emphasis was heavily placed on the teachings of the Bible. This foundation, while rich in scripture, was initially silent on the workings of miracles in our modern age. This silence broke dramatically for me as I began to witness events that defied logical explanation, moments that could only be understood as divine interventions. These miracles ranged from healings to profound personal encounters with God, each one peeling back the veil between heaven and earth just a little more.

Among the myriad experiences I've had, one stands out vividly: my own personal health crisis. A tumor nestled deep in my throat threatened not only my voice but my life's calling as a pastor. This period of suffering culminated in what I've come to describe as a "soul cry"—when you come to the end of yourself, you are ready for the beginning of God. It is a moment of utter vulnerability and desperate honesty before God. There's a scripture, "The Lord is near to all who call upon Him, To all who call upon Him in truth." (Psalm 145:18-19 NKJV)

In the instance of my health crisis, I was a confident young man called to ministry and now everything in my life felt as if it was falling apart. Although my honest cry for help was met initially with silence, it marked the beginning of a deep and personal experience and awareness of God's presence in my life. God led a pastor friend to reach out to me at just the right time with a needed word of encouragement. Miraculously, I emerged from surgery to find the tumor could not be located, a tangible sign of God's intervention. The surgeons had no explanation.

Both personally and as a pastor, I have also been marked by moments of waiting with God. This "waiting room" experience, as I've termed it, is not a denial of God's power but a deepening of our faith. It's in these periods of uncertainty and longing that we often find the most profound growth. I've seen how miraculous healings and divine interventions are not typically immediate but are always underpinned by a God who listens, who cares, and who acts in His perfect timing. It is important to remember that instant miracles are the exception. God's timing has a purpose that can be trusted. When we learn to trust Him and wait well, He empowers us and marks us with His character.

Other times God's answer to our prayer is a no on this side of heaven. As a pastor I have had the burden of grieving with people when God says no. I think the hardest instances of getting a no come after so many miracle prayers answered with a yes. Jesus Himself cried out while on the cross to His Father, "Why have you forsaken me?" (Matthew 27:46.) Although God did not answer, Luke 22:43 states that an angel appeared from heaven to strengthen Him. While it is perfectly okay to ask God why, my humble suggestion to anyone struggling with a painful no answer is to ask God, "How?" For example, "How am I going to get through this?" And the answer to this question is with the power of heaven. God will not allow us to avoid all suffering, but He will never ask you to suffer alone. We must learn to trust and worship God no matter what His plan is for our life. Ultimately death does not have the last word. Jesus does. Eternally speaking, you are getting a "wait."

The pinnacle of these miraculous "yes" experiences, and perhaps the most dramatic, occurred on a medical mission trip. To clarify, I have only seen God bring someone back from the dead once in my life. I don't think we should build our faith around these Lazarus-type miracles. Even so, we never know what God will do. We just have to believe in what He *can* do. I was on a medical mission trip in northern Vietnam. One of our doctors made a mistake with the child's airway. Despite exhaustive efforts, the child had not been breathing for 8 hours. I was called to scrub into the operating room to pray over the boy.

There was pandemonium and tension between the surgeons. I realized later that the doctors were worried they were going to go to jail. We were in communist Vietnam. We were a Christian organization. There were guards monitoring us constantly. I walk into the operating room in this third-world country to see this little boy on the operating room table naked and breathless.

The little guy was clearly dead. I remember my heart sinking. I felt so worthless and I was thinking in my head, *God what am I going to do here*? I felt enormous pressure. The one doctor from Texas screamed, "He's dead. Just call it!" Another doctor who was head of surgery calmly insisted, "Not until we pray. I am not calling it until we pray." I began to pray over this little boy. I just remember being so afraid to say amen. I was certain that God was going to say no. I had such little faith. And yet what does Jesus say, "If you have the faith of a mustard seed, you can move mountains." I can tell you I didn't have the faith of a mustard seed at that moment. That is how little faith God needs.

Just after I said amen, the little boy started urinating. I jumped back. Suddenly his little eyes open and he is looking at me. They scoop the little boy into their arms. The surgeon who made the error, not a believer but raised in church, had tears running down his face. He falls to the corner weeping and he says, "It's just like the stories in the Bible. It's just like the miracles my mom told me about."

This happened in a communist town. There is no God. Religion has been totally taken away from these people. Today, there is a church there. There is revival breaking out. God is moving and it is because this event happened in a place where people can't deny it. I still to this day am amazed that I got to witness this miracle. This is why we must pray out loud in Jesus' name. There is no other name under heaven by which man can be saved. The word saved in the Bible can be translated as "saved" or "healed," depending upon its context. The word is *sozo*. It means wholeness. It means healing.

This resurrection miracle, unique in my life's witnessing, underscores a fundamental truth: our faith is not in the miracles we seek but in the God we serve. This truth does not diminish the importance of miracles; rather, it places them in their proper context—as signs pointing us to the greater reality of God's kingdom.

Miracles, in my experience, are not just events that interrupt the natural order. They are divine messages, each one conveying a facet of God's love and sovereignty. They teach us, challenge us, and often change us, leaving indelible marks on our lives and communities. The miracle in Vietnam did more than bring a child back to life; it ignited a faith community in a place where the light of Christ was dim. Miracles matter because they are moments where heaven touches earth, where the impossible becomes possible, and where God reminds us of His presence and power.

In sharing these testimonies, my aim is not to sensationalize but to bear witness to a God who is alive and active in our world. The miracles I've seen, from personal healing to the awe-inspiring resurrection of a child, each serve to reinforce the truth that Jesus is the only name under heaven by which we can call upon for miracles. They remind us that while we may not always understand God's ways, we can always trust in His heart.

FURTHER REFLECTION

Matt Brown's journey into the miraculous showcases the profound power and presence of God in our lives. His experiences emphasize that miracles are divine messages, revealing God's love and sovereignty. Reflect on the moments in your life when you have witnessed or needed God's intervention. How can you deepen your faith and remain open to the miracles God can perform?

Imagine standing in a situation where you need a miracle, feeling the presence and power of God as Matt did. How can you nurture a faith that trusts in God's timing and purposes, even when answers seem delayed or different from what you expect?

PRAYER

Dear Heavenly Father,

Thank You for the miraculous testimonies shared by Matt Brown, which remind us of Your power and presence. Help me to trust in Your timing and to remain open to the miracles You can perform in my life. Strengthen my faith and guide me to rely on Your promises, knowing that You care for me deeply. Grant me the patience to wait for Your perfect timing and the courage to believe in Your ability to transform any situation. May my life reflect Your love and power, bringing hope and encouragement to those around me.

Amen.

CHAPTER 15
A GOSPEL ARTIST SURVIVES BRUTAL ATTACK AND RECEIVES POWERFUL MESSAGE FROM GOD

"But You, O Lord, are a shield for me,
My glory and the One who lifts up my head." **- Psalm 3:3 (NKJV)**

Tony Davis, a Gospel recording artist and pastor, fell victim to gang violence. Targeted for a gang initiation, he endured five gunshots that pierced his body making ten bullet holes, leaving him for dead on the streets of a Los Angeles neighborhood. However, divine intervention altered his fate. Tony's remarkable testimony encompasses his survival, a heavenly encounter, a miraculous healing of his voice and leg, an angelic visitation, and a divine calling that now guides his path. His compassionate spirit radiates through his story. The impactful work orchestrated by God through him is transforming and saving lives.- Julie

I am **Tony Davis**, and my life's trajectory changed drastically one evening in 2003, an event that not only tested my faith but also deepened it beyond measure. On what seemed like a routine day, I left my job, looking forward to picking up my wife, Chris, from her work at a boarding care facility for special-needs clients—a job we both loved and found fulfilling. Little did I know, I was about to encounter a trial that would transform my understanding of life.

As I neared the facility to pick up Chris, my Jeep was suddenly targeted and shot at by gang members. This abrupt violence was shocking; I had never had any conflicts in the neighborhood and had no reason to expect such an attack. In a desperate attempt to escape, I drove away quickly, only to realize the Jeep had been seriously damaged. I was forced to pull over, and it was then, in a moment of vulnerability, that the gravity of the situation truly hit me.

The next events unfolded like a nightmare. I found myself ambushed again, this time more directly. Bullets tore into my body, leaving me to grapple with pain and disbelief. The first bullet hit my right leg, and two more bullets followed. Amidst the chaos, a young gunman approached me with a gun drawn. He shot me two more times in my right side and my calf. I felt more bullets just missed my face and chest. I couldn't believe it. In that life-threatening moment, something profound happened.

Something deep inside me said to stand up and face my enemy. Despite my fear and the intense pain, a deep, spiritual instinct took over. Suddenly I saw the young man's eyes. His gun was pointed to my head. I said to him, "Why? What have I done to make you want to shoot me like this?" I invoked the name of Jesus, confronting my assailant with a plea for mercy that came from a place of faith deeper than I had ever known. **"In the name of Jesus, you aren't going to shoot me anymore."**

I know this statement was the power of God's Word rising up in my spirit. There is so much power to knowing God's Word and having it deep in your spirit. When I spoke the name of Jesus, his hands trembled. I saw a blackness clear from his eyes. He seemed to have a moment of clarity and he sank down. I heard him say, "My God what have I done?" I was left, wounded but alive, on the street. As I lay there, my physical life fading away, I felt as if demons were mocking me. I feared that maybe God abandoned me. Even so, at that moment I still trusted God. I lifted my hands and I began to worship Him. "God I love you. Just take care of my family."

I felt my heart slowing down. I knew I had lost so much blood, too much. I entered a state of clinical death. Right after I took my last breath, something wild happened. A female appeared. She looked familiar but I couldn't place her. Her hair was black and gray. I believe she was my guardian angel. She was all warmth and kindness, a real comfort after the craziness I'd just been through. She held my head in her lap and told me, "It's going to be alright," and I believed her. Her words calmed me down in a way I can't even explain.

Suddenly I felt like I was stepping out of my body, leaving behind the physical world for something way beyond normal. Imagine lying on the cold ground, and suddenly, you're floating up, feeling lighter by the second. As I moved upward I felt pain, sorrow and shame lifting off of me. But that was just the start. I kept moving up, drawn to this incredible light that made everything else seem dull in comparison. Through the clouds this huge window seemed to open and I saw a huge, beautiful city. I saw sparkles of light moving through the city. I felt the Holy Spirit speak to my spirit about the moving lights, "Those are archangels. They never stop praising God."

The closer I got, the more I felt this amazing love and peace wrapping around me, nothing like the pain and fear I'd felt before. I felt so free. I felt so loved. It was like stepping into a whole new world, a place so full of color and life, way more vivid than anything back on Earth. And the peace there? It was like nothing I'd ever felt-complete and total, wiping away every bit of pain or regret. To my left, I heard voices and felt so much joy. To my right, I felt peace and there was a waterfall. In the middle, I saw this beautiful golden glow. Clouds enveloped me and I felt the glory of God. I felt I was being held.

I felt I was with God Himself. I couldn't see Him, but His presence? It was undeniable, powerful beyond words. He had a message for me: **"Tony, it's not your time yet. Go back."** I desperately wanted to stay. I didn't want to leave this place of pure love. The next thing I heard has led me ever since, **"Tony, there's a message I need you to deliver to my people. Your work is not yet done."** I felt as if a hard wind was pushing me backward. I tried to grab something, anything to keep me in this place. Suddenly I breathed a deep breath. As I did that I found myself waking up in the hospital, a tube in my throat, with a man preparing to place a sheet over my head. I gave the man such a fright. He screamed and ran out of the room.

The staff told me I was clinically dead for 30 minutes. Initially, they told my wife that I might be brain-dead. The damage to my femoral artery in my right leg left me facing an above-the-knee amputation. One of my vocal cords was damaged when they placed an emergency tracheostomy. They weren't sure I would ever speak normally again. They proposed a possibility that I may be able to have a hole made in the side of my throat where I could use a device to help me speak. Given that my passion is singing Gospel music, this was horrific news. They moved me to the amputation room for the pending surgery.

Around midnight there was a change in the atmosphere of that hospital room. The Holy Spirit came into that room. He said one word to me, "Forgive." That one word was one of the most difficult things to hear in the aftermath of the events and trauma. I wrestled with God. "Look at what they did to me, God. I have never held a gun. I didn't deserve this." I began to think about forgiveness. As I looked at forgiveness I had the revelation that it is not based on feelings, but it is a decision God calls us to make. It releases us from the pain of what a situation has caused. Ultimately I knew God was calling me to forgive, and I told God I was going to choose forgiveness. "Lord, I forgive."

I pushed the pain and hurt out of my heart and I gave it to God. He took it and I felt free. I felt lighter. Somehow I knew He was going to take care of things. The room suddenly got warm. I felt something in my leg I can't explain but I knew God was working. Next, I felt the warmth in my throat. I felt things being mingled together. I lifted my hands and I said, "Jesus you said you would never leave me or forsake me. I trust you beyond my pain. You came here and touched me." I was so grateful.

Hours later I felt a sensation touching the bottom of my right foot, the leg they planned to amputate. I jumped and the doctors were shocked at how the leg looked and functioned. They rushed me to x-ray. They said, "We don't know what has happened, but there is life in that leg." They called me the miracle man. They wanted to evaluate my ability to speak after the damage to my vocal cord. They asked me to say something, anything, "Tony, take a deep breath and concentrate on pushing air upward." I took a deep breath and he adjusted the tube to see if I could speak. I said, "Jesus, my healer. Jesus, my deliverer." They were amazed. They removed the tube and closed up the hole in my throat.

My voice came back better. I came back whole. My leg is alive. I can jump. I can run. All the things that the enemy tried to steal, God gave it all back and He doubled it. He has called me to share this message of the power of forgiveness. I experienced a profound moment of healing in my body. This was not just physical healing, but a deep, spiritual restoration that compelled me to forgive those who had harmed me. This act of forgiveness was not borne out of weakness but from a place of divine conviction. It was a pivotal moment that set the course for my recovery and my life's mission henceforth.

My miraculous recovery confounded the medical professionals and became a testament to the power of faith and forgiveness. Despite being told I would never walk again, let alone survive without severe cognitive impairments, I defied every prediction. My journey of healing was marked by significant milestones, not just in my physical recovery but in the spiritual revelations and the purpose that was revealed to me.

Months after the accident I felt compelled to go back to the scene to find the young gang members. I wanted to save their souls by leading them to Jesus. I arrived to find yellow caution tape around the house where the gang members lived. I stood with my Bible in hand wondering what had happened. This homeless man came out of nowhere, limping and pushing a cart. He approached me, "Are those your people?" He shared with me that there was a huge gang fight and all of the men had died. "Oh really? Oh man, I came to forgive. Why God, why?" I said with disappointment. The homeless man was quick to reply, "The forgiveness was for you!" I turned to reply to him and he was gone. I ran around the corner and I couldn't see this man anywhere. He completely disappeared. I believe this man was an angel.

In the years that followed, I dedicated myself to sharing the message of hope, forgiveness, and divine purpose. My testimony took on various forms: speaking engagements, a book, and even a film. Each platform allowed me to reach out to those in need of hearing that there is a greater plan, a divine purpose that can emerge from the depths of despair and suffering.

The essence of my message revolves around the power of forgiveness —a principle that was not only pivotal in my healing but also in my spiritual growth. Forgiveness, as I learned, is not a sign of weakness but a courageous act of liberation. It frees one from the chains of anger, resentment, and pain, allowing God's love to heal and restore. This realization has been the cornerstone of my outreach, guiding my efforts to heal, inspire, and transform lives through the grace of God.

My life, post-recovery, has been a testament to the limitless potential of faith in action. Through the National Increase Peace Foundation, I've been able to contribute positively to communities, advocating for peace and reconciliation. The foundation's work, alongside my personal mission, aims to foster environments where love and forgiveness can flourish, where individuals are inspired to overcome adversity through faith.

As I share my testimony, I do so with a heart full of gratitude and a spirit committed to serving others. My experience, while uniquely mine, carries a universal message of resilience, hope, and the transformative power of divine love. It is a call to each of us to embrace our journey, to find strength in our faith, and to open our hearts to the healing grace of forgiveness. In doing so, we not only liberate ourselves but also light the way for others, contributing to a world where love triumphs over hate, peace overcomes violence, and faith dispels fear.

FURTHER REFLECTION

Tony Davis' testimony is a powerful reminder of the transformative power of faith and forgiveness. His experience illustrates how, even in the face of life-threatening violence, invoking the name of Jesus and choosing to forgive can lead to miraculous healing and restoration. Reflect on the areas in your life where you may be holding onto pain, resentment, or fear. How can you open your heart to the power of forgiveness and allow God's healing love to transform you?

Imagine yourself in Tony's situation, facing seemingly insurmountable challenges and yet choosing to trust in God's power. How can you cultivate a deeper faith that allows you to forgive and experience the fullness of God's grace in your life?

PRAYER

Dear Heavenly Father,

Thank You for the inspiring testimony of Tony Davis, which shows the power of faith and forgiveness. Help me to trust in Your healing power and to choose forgiveness, even when it is difficult. Strengthen my faith and guide me to rely on Your promises, knowing that Your love and grace can transform any situation. Grant me the courage to forgive those who have wronged me and to embrace the freedom that comes from Your healing touch. May my life reflect Your love and power, bringing hope and encouragement to those around me.

Amen.

CHAPTER 16

AGAINST ALL ODDS: A-TWO-YEAR OLD'S MIRACLE HEALING AFTER A DEVASTATING ACCIDENT

"But they that wait upon the LORD shall renew their strength;
they shall mount up with wings as eagles; they shall run,
and not be weary; and they shall walk, and not faint."
- Isaiah 40:31 (NKJV)

Precious Micah was only two years old when he suffered an internal decapitation after a car accident. In the words of his neurosurgeon, "This is the worst injury we could imagine." One skilled neurologist advised the most humane option would be to discontinue care. John and Heather suddenly found themselves in a crucible where their faith would be tested and ultimately sustain them. - Julie

My name's **John Andrews**, and I've got a testimony to share about my son, Micah, that's both harrowing and hopeful. It all began on what seemed like an ordinary day, a day that quickly took an unexpected and nearly tragic turn for our family. I was at work, planning to sneak in some fishing afterwards since I had my boat with me. Heather, my wife, was out shopping with a friend instead of the usual Wednesday church visit with the kids. They were all buckled up in the car, safe and sound, or so we thought.

On their way back home, our world turned upside down. Their car was hit broadside at 50 miles an hour. The impact was on Micah and Heather's side. As fate would have it, I drove past the accident scene without a clue that my own family was involved. I was just hoping the delay wouldn't be too long.

Not long after, I got a call. It was a firefighter telling me to rush to the hospital. He tried to reassure me by saying, "We did everything we could." You hear that, and your heart just sank. I couldn't fathom what lay ahead.

When I arrived at the hospital, the reality of the situation hit me like a ton of bricks. Micah had been internally decapitated-a term I wish I never learned. It means his skull was detached from his spine, a condition as grim as it sounds. The doctors, they weren't optimistic. They said 98.5 percent of people with this injury don't make it, and the lucky few who do... well, they're typically paralyzed and wheelchair bound. Christopher Reeves was one of those miracle cases.

Despite the overwhelming odds, Heather and I, we just couldn't give up hope. There was this unshakable feeling inside both of us that Micah was going to pull through, that God was watching over him. And so began our vigil by his bedside, day in and day out, praying, hoping, believing. Heather reflected back to the scene with gratitude how God clearly led her to gently hold up Micah's head in alignment. We knew He was with us.

Dr. Theodore, God bless him, was the surgeon who took on Micah's case. He performed this incredible surgery, attaching Micah's skull back to his spine with a piece of titanium and a bit of Micah's own rib. It was groundbreaking, and it was our first glimmer of hope. Dr. Theodore was the world-leading expert for this surgery. He developed the surgery.

In the days that followed, we clung to every positive sign, no matter how small. The first news after surgery was that Micah was paralyzed and we, have to wait to see about his brain function. It was brutal. I have always been taught to have faith, that God is in control, but I was so afraid to fully surrender my child to God in fear that God's will would be to take him. There were moments of despair, sure, but there was a big moment that we knew God was sending us a sign of hope.

The neurologist came to share the negative results of the brain scan and the damage that had occurred. One of the residents in tow met eyes with my father-in-law, "Alex?!" The resident replied, "Craig?" The resident was a doctor from Slovakia who Craig met as a child in a youth group at a church he planted years ago in a small Slovak village. Alex was the one believer on that medical team. We all instantly knew, given the odds of this reunion, that God is sovereign and so completely in control! Alex would pray with us and this became the pivotal moment where things started to change for the better. I finally surrendered Micah to God, trusting His will, that He is in control after this confirmation of His presence.

They told us our son would be paralyzed and that his brain would likely have severe permanent damage. They wanted to arrange for a wheelchair. My wife Heather had not left the hospital and was at her lowest point when God sent a nurse. This woman set aside everything and prayed heaven down to Earth over my wife. It was the most incredibly powerful prayer my wife had ever heard. It was a perfectly timed blessing she will never forget. God kept prompting me to keep our eyes on Him, not the waves of our storm. He kept sending people into our path to comfort and support us.

On day twelve they decided to try to wake Micah and we were praying, hanging on to hope for any kind of activity. He opened his eyes. It was amazing and heartbreaking at the same time. His first response was he growled and was not himself, but he briefly drew up his limbs. We were simultaneously bawling and ecstatic. He wasn't paralyzed! Later I whispered 'diaper' to Micah, a silly family inside joke, and he grinned. That grin was everything. It was Micah telling us, 'I'm still here.' It was the first real sign that his brain was working. He had so much to overcome, but this was a major victory.

Micah's recovery was nothing short of miraculous. Slowly but surely, he defied every odd stacked against him. He started moving, responding, and before we knew it, he was on the path to recovery. It wasn't easy, mind you. There was therapy, lots of it, and there were setbacks, but Micah, he's a fighter. And all along the way God sent people to bless us.

Five or six months later, Heather and Micah were walking to rehab through the hospital skybridge when they met the eyes of the skilled neurologist and his team. A non-believer, this was the same doctor who had advised us to discontinue treatment for Micah. Micah smiled and reached out his hand to say hello and the doctor was speechless as he realized who he was. "**God is good**," Heather shared warmly. We are hopeful that Micah's miracle may have opened this talented doctor's mind and heart for God to move in his life.

Dr. Theodore, the outstanding surgeon God provided for Micah, is a man of faith. Reflecting on Micah's journey, he shared with the family, "I may have fixed Micah's neck, but I didn't heal him. Miracles happen every day," giving God the glory. We will be forever grateful for the medical care we received from everyone.

Looking back, I see how this journey tested our faith, reshaped it, even. It showed us the power of hope, the strength that comes from a community rallying around you, and most importantly, the unwavering love of a family. So many say that God won't give you more than you can handle. Well, I can tell you that He will at times give you way more than you can handle. He wants you to rely on and trust in Him. You have to learn to lean on Him and walk by faith and not by sight.

Today, Micah's doing great. You wouldn't know what he's been through just by looking at him. He's on track with school, loves shooting hoops, and has this zest for life that's infectious. Sure, there are challenges, but when I look at Micah, I see a living, breathing miracle.

Through every step of this journey, we've witnessed the profound impact of God's grace. It's a force that's difficult to articulate but impossible to ignore. This grace didn't just guide the surgeon's hands or spark the first signs of Micah's recovery; it was present in every moment of despair, offering us strength when our own was waning. In the darkest hours, it was God's grace that reminded us we were not alone, that our prayers were heard, and that even in the face of overwhelming odds, there was a path forward. It taught us that grace isn't just about miraculous healing; it's found in the support of our community, the resilience of our son, and the unwavering bond of our family. God's grace showed us that even when the future seems uncertain, faith can illuminate the way through any storm. Micah's story, marked by both hardship and hope, is a testament to the boundless grace that surrounds us, teaches us, and ultimately, transforms us.

FURTHER REFLECTION

John's testimony about his son Micah highlights the power of faith, hope, and community in the face of overwhelming challenges. When faced with seemingly insurmountable odds, the family's unwavering trust in God and the support from those around them led to a miraculous recovery. This story reminds us that God is present even in our darkest moments, working through others to provide comfort and strength. Reflect on your own life and consider how you can lean more on your faith and the community around you during tough times.

Take a moment to imagine God's presence in your own challenges. How can you surrender your fears and trust in His plan, even when the path seems unclear? Consider the ways God might be using those around you to provide support and encouragement.

PRAYER

Dear Heavenly Father,

Thank You for the powerful testimony of John and Micah, which shows the incredible impact of faith and community. Help me to trust in Your divine plan, even when the future seems uncertain. Grant me the strength to rely on You fully, knowing that Your grace and love are always present. Guide me to be a source of support and encouragement for others, just as You have placed people in my life to uplift me. Strengthen my faith and help me to see Your hand at work in every situation. May I always remember that with You, all things are possible.

Amen.

CHAPTER 17
A HOLLYWOOD STUNTMAN
SURVIVES THE IMPOSSIBLE

"Therefore, if anyone is in Christ, he is a new creation; old things have passed away; behold, all things have become new."
- 2 Corinthians 5:17 (NKJV)

A Hollywood stuntman's survival after being crushed by a 10-ton truck with 25 people in the truck bed is just one of the many miracles in William's life. I was so touched by William's deep longing for something more, and how a very personal God met him in his mess. William has a passion to reveal the transformational love of Jesus to others and has blessed many by sharing his miracle testimony in his free online books and in his speaking engagements. - Julie

I am **William Harper**. From a young age, I felt there was something missing from my life. There was a deep longing I yearned to fill. Growing up I had an extraordinary passion for motorcycles. It was more than just a hobby for me; it felt like my calling. I dove into motocross racing, and by the time I was 15, I was already competing. I quickly climbed the ranks and even won a couple of championships. I thought the wins and recognition would be more fulfilling, but they weren't.

The high of racing felt amazing. The rush of speeding past the finish line, the crowd's roar-that was my world, my identity. But then, like a series of dominoes tumbling down, injuries began to pile up, each one a brutal reminder that my dreams were slipping through my fingers. I went from being on top of the world to watching my world crumble around me. Each injury, each setback, felt like a personal failure. My body, once a symbol of success and strength, became a constant source of pain and frustration. It was as if every broken bone, every scar, was a mark of my fall from grace.

In the depths of this despair, I turned to cocaine. It promised an escape, a way to numb the pain, both physical and emotional. But the highs were fleeting, and the lows became unbearable. A minor stint in jail for drug-related offenses should have been a wake-up call, but it wasn't. Instead, it pushed me further into the abyss. I was on a path of self-destruction, and I couldn't see a way out.

Seeking a fresh start, I ventured into the world of stunt work. The transition from the dirt tracks to the film sets of Hollywood seemed like a new beginning. I found success, even doubling for Sylvester Stallone, an achievement that would be a dream come true for many. But my past demons were never far behind. During the filming of *The River* in Alabama, a straightforward stunt turned into a nightmare. I landed incorrectly and was crushed under a 10-ton truck holding 25 people. The rear dual tires drove over my neck and chest. I can still hear the horrific sound of my bones breaking. I briefly lost consciousness, seeing only white and I couldn't move at first. I just knew I was dead. There was no way a human body could handle that, but somehow I kept breathing. Miraculously, in spite of a broken neck, broken ribs, broken shoulder blades and internal damage, I survived. But this brush with death left me with more questions than answers. Why was I spared? What was the purpose of my survival?

My recovery was a long and painful journey. When I returned to the set, people were shocked to see me alive. My survival was an undeniable miracle witnessed by everyone on set, but it was the words of two very serious individuals I had never seen before that truly struck me. They spoke of a divine purpose behind my survival, a notion I initially dismissed. **"You were dead. God kept you alive for a reason. He has plans for you."** Their words lingered in my mind, a haunting suggestion that there was more to my life than what I had seen. Who were these men?

Despite this glimmer of hope, the pull of addiction proved too strong. Despite a brief period of financial success and a great job, I fell back into the clutches of drugs, unsatisfied. This time it was due to cocaine. The following years were a blur of addiction, criminal activities, and a constant fight for survival. I met a woman and pulled loved ones into the chaos. We led a nomadic existence, always trying to stay one step ahead of the law, but our luck eventually ran out in Montana. My partner and I faced serious legal charges, a culmination of years of running from our problems. Facing the possibility of a 100-year sentence was a reality check like no other. It was the wake-up call I couldn't ignore, a realization of how far I had fallen and the long road to redemption that lay ahead.

When my life seemed like it couldn't get any lower, something extraordinary happened. While hiding out from the authorities, I had an open vision from God. As we were driving, I saw myself at a gas station ahead being arrested as if it were on a television screen. As we approached this gas station the driver was planning to stop for gas. I told her, "I can't go there! I am going to get arrested." I had an idea to escape and hide in the woods adjacent to the gas station. As I looked to the side to get out and flee, something supernatural happened. Everything in that direction became like a curtain of utter blackness. I have done some scary stunts, but the feeling I had with this darkness was the most terrifying thing I had ever experienced. I had no choice but to go to the gas station. Sure enough, the scene played out exactly as the vision God had shown me.

For the first time, I knew this was God intervening. It gave me an odd peace which I didn't normally have when I was being arrested. I said to God, "I always believed in You, but I never thought You were this personal to care about a person like me. You tell me what to do and I will do it. I am all Yours." I was not expecting what came next. God clearly said to me, **"Read the Bible."** It couldn't have been more clear if it were a red neon blinking sign in a hotel lobby flashing in my face.

Alone in my prison cell, wrestling with the reality of possibly spending the rest of my life behind bars. I reflected on the vision. I remembered the two serious men, possibly angels, who told me that God had a purpose for my life. This wasn't some abstract, feel-good message; it was a direct, life-altering encounter. I was shown that my life, as messed up as it was, had a purpose. God's message was clear: read the Bible. Now, for a guy like me, who had spent years running from anything that even remotely smelled like authority or rules, this was a tall order. The Bible? Really? That ancient book I thought had no relevance to someone like me? But in that cell, with nowhere else to turn, I decided to give it a shot.

Reading the Bible in jail wasn't just an activity to pass the time; it was my lifeline. The words jumped off the page, speaking directly to my heart and situation. It was as if God was using every verse, every story, to rewrite the narrative of my life. The anger, the bitterness, and the pain that had fueled my descent into drugs and crime began to dissipate. In their place, I found forgiveness, healing, and a peace I'd never known. The deep inner longing I had tried to fill with adrenaline, trophies, money, and drugs was finally met in a personal relationship with God. I was in jail and facing 100 years in prison, but I had finally found the only thing that satisfied the deep inner longing. I had complete peace.

It was a process, but God would show his favor by shortening my time in jail. He would continue to transform my life from the inside out. He gave me a new identity. I was no longer just William Harper, the stuntman, the convict, the addict. I was a child of God, loved, forgiven, and set on a new path. My past mistakes became the foundation for a future ministry, a way to help others find the same hope and redemption that had been gifted to me.

Looking back, I realize that every moment, even the darkest ones, was leading me to find true freedom and peace. My path was not easy, but it was necessary for me to become the person I am today. As I continue to walk this new path, I do so with the knowledge that I'm never alone, that my story is part of a larger story of hope, renewal, and grace. Thank you for listening to my testimony. May it be a reminder that no one is beyond the reach of transformation, and it's never too late to turn toward the light and find a new beginning. I continue to share my testimony and the love of Jesus everywhere I can and give away my books. I am still writing poetry and sharing the hope and healing that is available in Jesus.

FURTHER REFLECTION

William Harper's journey demonstrates that even in our darkest moments, there is hope for transformation and redemption. His story of overcoming addiction, injury, and imprisonment through a personal encounter with God serves as a powerful reminder that no one is beyond God's reach. Reflect on areas of your life where you might feel trapped or hopeless. Consider how turning to God and immersing yourself in His word can bring about profound change and healing.

Imagine your own struggles and burdens being lifted by a higher power. How can you open your heart to God's guidance and embrace the possibility of a new beginning? Reflect on the idea that God has a purpose for your life, even if it is not immediately clear.

PRAYER

Dear Lord,

Thank You for the incredible transformation in William Harper's life. Help me to trust in Your plans for my life, even when I feel lost or hopeless. Guide me to seek You and find peace in Your presence. Grant me the strength to overcome my struggles and the wisdom to see Your purpose in my journey. May I find comfort and direction in Your word, and may Your love and grace fill every corner of my life. Let my life be a testament to Your power to heal, restore, and renew. Thank You for never giving up on me and for always being by my side.

Amen.

CHAPTER 18
A FAMILY REUNION IN HEAVEN AND ON EARTH

"For by grace you have been saved through faith-and this is not from yourselves, it is the gift of God, not byworks, so that no one can boast."
- Ephesians 2:8-9 (NIV)

Ken was an air traffic controller who nearly died of the H1N1 flu. As his comatose body was on the brink of death, his sister cried out to God to bring him back with a powerful testimony. God answered her prayer. Ken got a glimpse of heaven and came back with a powerful message that will bless each of us. Ken and his wife Hatsy have been blessed and they love to share the love of God with people everywhere they go! - Julie

I am **Ken Johnson**. I was saved when I was about 12 years old. Although I've always been a Christian, I wasn't deeply involved in religious activities due to my shift work as an air traffic controller. My wife took our sons to church regularly, but I often couldn't attend. Despite reading parts of the Bible, my knowledge was more academic than heartfelt.

In the mid-70s, during my service in the Army, we were mandated to take a flu vaccine. Unfortunately, the vaccine contained a live virus, and I became extremely ill. This incident was documented in my permanent record as an allergy to the flu vaccine, which was not the case. Years later, at 58, I fell seriously ill again. It began with a sore throat on a Tuesday, and by the following Tuesday, my wife had to call 911. I was admitted to the hospital and placed directly into the ICU.

My condition was severe; I had H1N1, which progressed to pneumonia and then to acute respiratory distress syndrome (ARDS). With only a 5 percent survival rate for ARDS, I faced a dire situation. I was hospitalized for a total of 84 days and spent an additional 42 days in a rehab unit. When I finally returned home, I was very weak, having lost 80 pounds and was only able to walk a few steps with a walker.

During my hospital stay, I experienced numerous complications. I was put on a ventilator and feeding tube, developed deep vein thrombosis, and had a severe reaction to heparin called heparin-induced thrombocytopenia, leading to a low platelet blood count. These complications brought me close to death multiple times.

At one point, my condition was so critical that my family was called in, being told the next 48 hours were crucial. My brother in Tennessee and my sister in Georgia both felt my presence with them simultaneously. When my sister sensed the grim nature of my condition, she began to cry out to God. She asked God to send me back with a powerful testimony to share with others. This reinforced my belief in the reality of what I experienced during my illness.

In one of the darkest moments, I had a profound near-death experience. I found myself in a dark place with a single red flower on the ground, which I was told I had to decide if I would eat or not eat. The voice said it was sweet as honey but bitter in your stomach.

Following this, I was in a beautiful place filled with flowers of indescribable colors, with a huge tree in front of me and a radiant white light emanating overwhelming love and peace. It was a feeling of love that was powerful it would make you cry. A voice, which I believe was God, conveyed a message of love and reassurance. Without words, He communicated clearly to me, **"I love you more than you will ever, ever know and I have you in my right hand."**

My deceased brother, Ricky, appeared to me, looking much younger and wearing a white t-shirt, and told me I had to return. Although I wanted to stay in that beautiful place, I was reassured that I would be okay upon returning.

When I woke up from the coma, I was strapped to the bed to prevent me from removing the ventilator. This period was incredibly emotional, as I couldn't move or speak, and I often cried. However, a sense of peace assured me I would recover. My wife read to me from a devotional book, *Jesus Calling*, which provided daily encouragement.

Five years later, I have about 50.6 percent lung capacity and can only walk for short periods. Despite these physical limitations, my experience has profoundly changed me. Before my illness, I rarely shared my faith, but now, I feel compelled to tell my story.

During a visit to my mother in Knoxville, Tennessee, I experienced a moment of divine timing. My mother, who was 88 years old at the time, had been worried about me since I had been very sick and living far away. The pulmonologist arranged for me to travel with a portable oxygen tank so I could visit her. This trip was also an opportunity to mend the strained relationship with my brother, with whom I hadn't spoken in two and a half years.

Before the trip, I texted my brother to let him know I was coming to see our mom and to express my desire to reconcile and catch up. However, I didn't receive any response from him. Despite this, my wife and I set off for Knoxville, arriving on a Thursday afternoon.

Once there, my mother suggested we go out for dinner early, as she usually preferred. As we were discussing where to go, I suddenly felt a strong, almost urgent prompting to go to Cracker Barrel. It was an unusual and insistent feeling, one that I couldn't ignore. I suggested Cracker Barrel to my mom, and she agreed enthusiastically.

We drove to Cracker Barrel, and as we arrived, my wife opened the door to the restaurant's vestibule. At that exact moment, my estranged brother was opening the inner door. Our eyes met in surprise. He was supposed to be at work, but he had stopped by Cracker Barrel to get some chicken soup for his wife, who was unwell. The timing of our meeting felt too precise to be a coincidence.

It became clear to me that God had orchestrated this encounter. My mother, witnessing the unexpected reunion, looked at me and said, "God did that." We hugged, talked, and cried, sharing a deeply emotional moment. Although our relationship isn't as close as I'd like it to be, we began to communicate again after that meeting. This encounter was a profound reminder of God's presence and His ability to bring people together in the most unexpected ways.

My minister and my brother helped me find biblical references to my experiences, particularly in Revelation 10 and Ezekiel 3, which described similar visions. Both passages speak of a scroll from an angel that is sweet like honey in your mouth and bitter in your stomach. I believe this flower I saw in heaven represents the Gospel of Jesus. I had never read this in the Bible. This validation strengthened my faith and affirmed the reality of my near-death experience.

Through all these experiences, I've learned to live each day with gratitude and purpose, spreading kindness and sharing my story to inspire others. I continue to see God's hand in my life, even in everyday interactions, such as a phone conversation where I unknowingly prevented someone from taking their life.

Ultimately, my journey has reaffirmed my belief in God's love and presence. Even with ongoing health challenges, I trust in His plan and strive to be a testimony of His grace and mercy.

FURTHER REFLECTION

Ken Johnson's story reveals the power of faith and the presence of God during our darkest times. Facing life-threatening illness, Ken experienced profound moments that strengthened his belief in God's love and purpose. Reflect on how, even in our struggles, we can find God's guiding hand and reassurance. Consider how you can deepen your relationship with God and trust in His plans, especially when faced with adversity.

Imagine yourself in a situation where you need God's guidance and love. How can you open your heart to feel His presence and listen to His voice? Reflect on the times when you felt alone and how, through faith, you can find strength and comfort in God's promises.

PRAYER

Dear Lord,

Thank You for Your unwavering presence and love, even in our most challenging times. Help us to trust in Your plans and to find comfort in Your guiding hand. Give us the strength to face our struggles with faith and the courage to share our stories to inspire others. May we always remember that Your love is greater than we can ever comprehend and that You hold us in Your right hand. Guide us each day to live with gratitude and purpose, spreading kindness and sharing Your message of hope. We thank You for Your grace and mercy, and we pray that we may always feel Your presence in our lives.

Amen.

CHAPTER 19

MIRACULOUS REDEMPTION AND DIVINE ORCHESTRATION OF A KIDNEY TRANSPLANT

*"He brought them out of darkness, the utter darkness,
and broke away their chains."*
- Psalm 107:14 (NIV)

———————

Jocelynn was on the most-wanted list and had an addiction to drugs that was out of control. Only God could have written this testimony of complete transformation. Her surrender and obedience to God has saved not only her life, but countless others. Miracles in this phenomenal testimony include deliverance, addiction recovery, healing, restoration and a divinely orchestrated kidney transplant! God has positioned her for such a time as this! I can't wait to see what He does next through this beautiful spirited woman! - Julie

My name is **Jocelynn James Edmonds**, hailing from East Franklin, Alabama, and my testimony is one of profound change, redemption, and divine intervention. It's a narrative that found its way onto the cover of the May 2021 Guidepost magazine, graced television screens more times than I can count, and unfolded in writings that have reached count-less hearts. At the heart of my tale is a miraculous deliverance from addic-tion, a second chance at life, and an extraordinary act of kindness that bridged my past with an unforeseen future.

My descent into darkness was rapid and devastating. A series of surg-eries and prescription medications opened the door for an addiction. Within a span of five years, I accumulated 16 felonies, driven by a despera-tion to feed my addiction. Life had whittled down to a relentless pursuit of the next high, stealing anything I could lay my hands on, and navigating the chaos of being a single mother to two precious children. By 2011, my existence had spiraled into homelessness, loss, and despair. I had hit rock bottom. Seeing my face plastered across the television screen as Franklin County's most wanted was the jolt I needed to confront the ruin my life had become. It was at my lowest moment that I experienced a profound moment of clarity: I was sick and tired of being sick and tired.

The decision to turn myself in marked the beginning of a grueling journey toward redemption. Detoxing in jail over the holiday season, away from my children, was a harrowing experience. Yet, it was during this time that I realized that rehabilitation wasn't merely about escaping addiction; it was about confronting and transforming the very essence of who I was. The world's largest rehab for women became my crucible for change. It was there, amidst the struggles and introspection, that I surrendered my life to God, marking a pivotal moment of true conversion and deliverance. My healing was not instant, it was a process.

Emerging from rehabilitation, I was a changed woman, armed with newfound sobriety and a deep commitment to serve others. Yet, it was a series of divine revelations that set the stage for an even more extraordinary chapter in my life. One day, I came across a social media post about a man in dire need of a kidney transplant. As I read, the Holy Spirit communicated to me—not audibly, but as a clear and authoritative voice within my thoughts—that I was the match for this man's kidney. Initially, I resisted, telling God I didn't have time for this. However, deep inside, I knew God had chosen me as a match.

After praying and fasting, seeking a clear confirmation, I woke with the scripture "Love thy neighbor" in my heart. Compelled, I reached out to the man's daughter who had posted the plea, telling her, "I have your dad's kidney. Just tell me what I have to do." Despite the odds, after undergoing the necessary tests—arranged without informing anyone—I received the call confirming I was a perfect match. It was a miracle; despite my past drug use, my kidneys were in perfect health, making me an ideal donor. In fact, the match was so perfect that the medical team at Vanderbilt initially thought I was the man's daughter. The transplant set a record for the highest urine output post-operation, marking a success beyond medical expectations. This sequence of events didn't just lead to a successful kidney transplant but also fostered an unlikely yet profoundly beautiful friendship with the police officer who had arrested me three times during my years of turmoil. This revelation, as shocking as it was divine, illustrates the mysterious and miraculous ways God works in our lives, turning our past struggles into testimonies of hope and renewal.

The journey didn't end there. I emerged from jail and rehab with nothing but a clear vision from God for a facility and ministry and a conviction to help others to get free. I embarked on a mission to aid those battling addiction. My efforts have seen over a thousand individuals find their way to treatment, fueled by my unwavering commitment and the support of a community that believes in second chances. The vision for the Place of Grace, a facility dedicated to recovery and healing, is slowly coming to fruition, a testament to the transformative power of faith, perseverance, and the kindness of strangers.

As I reflect on this journey, it's clear that my life is a tapestry of miracles, woven by a higher power that saw potential in my brokenness. The path from addiction to redemption, from receiving mercy to extending it in the most profound way, has been nothing short of miraculous. The friendship with the officer, the lives touched by my testimony, and the dreams unfolding before me are vivid reminders that hope is real, change is possible, and our lives can be instruments of divine grace.

I'm overwhelmed with gratitude for each moment that has led me here. The journey ahead is filled with the promise of new beginnings, the joy of transformed lives, and a steadfast belief in the miracles that enrich our daily existence. The Place of Grace, a vision God entrusted to me, took root as a ministry in 2013 and has since flourished into a testament to faith and communal support. Following a generous land donation from a local church in 2021, by 2022 we celebrated the construction of our facility. Though the interior is still under enhancement, this space has profoundly impacted the lives of 2,896 women, and this number is steadily growing. Alongside me in this endeavor is my husband Greg, who serves as the president and on the board of directors, helping to steer The Place of Grace toward fulfilling its mission. Our journey together at The Place of Grace stands as living evidence of God's incredible work, highlighting the remarkable outcomes that emerge when we answer His call and dedicate ourselves to serving others with compassion and commitment.

FURTHER REFLECTION

Jocelynn James Edmonds' journey from addiction to redemption high-lights the power of surrender, faith, and divine intervention. Her transformation began with a moment of clarity and a decision to seek help. Despite the challenges, her faith guided her toward a path of healing and service. Reflect on how surrendering your struggles to God can lead to profound change and new purpose. Consider how God might be calling you to use your experiences to help others and spread hope.

Imagine yourself in a moment of despair, feeling God's presence and hearing His call to trust Him. How can you open your heart to His guidance and find the strength to overcome your challenges? Reflect on the ways God might be using your journey to impact others positively.

PRAYER

Dear Lord,

Thank You for Your unwavering presence and the transformative power of Your love. Help us to surrender our struggles to You, trusting in Your plan for our lives. Guide us as we seek healing and redemption, and use our experiences to inspire and help others. Strengthen our faith, and fill us with the courage to follow

Your call, even when the path seems difficult. May our lives be a testament to Your grace and mercy, and may we always find hope in Your promises. Grant us the wisdom to see Your hand in our journey and the compassion to extend Your love to those in need.

Amen.

CHAPTER 20
A CHILD EXPERIENCES MIRACLE HEALING AND JESUS

" Though I walk in the midst of trouble, You will revive me;
You will stretch out Your hand against the wrath of my enemies,
And Your right hand will save me. "
- Psalm 138:7 (NKJV

Mike and Melissa's faith is tested as they face the reality of losing their precious four-year-old daughter Mia. A fun family hike in God's beautiful creation takes a terrifying turn when Mia sustains fatal injuries from a massive falling tree branch. God's fingerprints are laced throughout this powerful testimony, leading up to the unexpected blessing of Mia sharing her experiences with Jesus in heaven! Praising God with this family! -Julie

I'm **Mike Harris**, and alongside my wife Melissa, I want to share the extraordinary story of our daughter Mia, whose life was nearly taken from us and then miraculously returned in a series of events that can only be described as divine intervention.

Our story begins in October of 2020, amidst the sprawling beauty of

Hocking Hills, Ohio. It was our last full day there, and we decided to take our children on a hike to enjoy the great outdoors. The day was perfect, the hike was breathtaking, and little did we know, our lives were about to change forever. As the hike neared its end, tragedy struck in the form of a falling branch. A large branch fell from approximately 60 feet, hitting Mia directly in the head and leaving her unconscious. In that moment, panic set in. Holding Mia, lifeless in my arms, I feared the worst. Melissa, hearing my shout, rushed over, and together we faced every parent's nightmare: the possibility of losing our child.

With no cell service in the dense woods and our daughter in critical condition, I felt a desperation I've never known. However, in my most desperate moment, I remembered the emergency SOS feature on my phone. Miraculously, it worked, and I was connected to a 911 operator with crystal-clear service, a first glimmer of hope that perhaps we were not alone in this.

Back at the scene, Melissa was doing everything she could to comfort Mia, praying fervently for a miracle. Our prayers were desperate, our hearts were breaking, and yet, there was a part of us that was already preparing to let Mia go, trying to find peace in the belief that she would be with Jesus. My thoughts bounced from believing for a miracle to wondering if I would be faced with officiating Mia's funeral the following week. It was a chaotic time for us, and we found ourselves completely submitted to the Lord.

The passage in scripture about the woman with the issue of blood, touching Jesus' garment to be healed came to Melissa as she waited for help. "Lord, there is that much power in you that this woman simply touched the hem of your garment and was healed. If your power lives in me through the Holy Spirit, then you have the power to heal Mia." Melissa laid her hands on Mia and prayed that prayer over and over again.

The ambulance's arrival felt like an eternity, but help did arrive. Melissa stayed close to the ambulance and I answered questions of the investigating officer. There was a moment between us as Mia was finally in the hands of the paramedics. Melissa was pacing with emotion and turned to me as the reality hit. We felt we were about to lose our daughter. Where were we going to stand with the Lord in a moment like this? Melissa needed to know that our faith would be enough to sustain us in this storm. This would be a moment for us to stand firm together, acknowledging we are trusting the Lord regardless. He is everything to us.

God blessed us with people that would help take care of our other children so we could be with Mia. News began to spread about the accident quickly and prayers for Mia were now being lifted up by people around the country. We were so grateful for those prayers.

The paramedics couldn't offer hope but worked tirelessly. Eventually, Mia was taken to the hospital. The medical staff was persistent, but the situation was grim. They didn't think she'd make it. However, Mia's condition began to improve against all odds. Each small sign of progress felt like a monumental victory, from the neurosurgeon's announcement that no immediate surgery was needed to Mia's miraculous recovery over the following days.

Mia had five compression fractures in her spine and injuries to her brain. They wanted to allow the swelling to go down as they monitored her and a machine helped her breathe. The next day they decided to see if she could breathe on her own and they pulled out the breathing tube. We were guarded but so hopeful. Finally we heard, "I pee'd in my pull up." We knew we were not out of the woods, but this was a big victory. Recovery was a process, but we had hope.

Once Mia was more stable, the doctor did see an area of her skull that needed surgery. This surgery ended up being much more than expected, as her skull was fractured severely. The timing of this finding and repair was critical in her healing process. This was the first time in this journey I began to get angry. The roller coaster of the ups and downs was so challenging. To come so far with improvement and hear more scary news was difficult. Even so, God continued to work and move in ways we couldn't imagine.

Mia's journey from the brink of death back to us was nothing short of a miracle. She not only survived but began to thrive. Mia had no seizures and has no deficits. She has come through with flying colors, her spirit and strength shining brighter than ever. Mia's recovery was rapid and remarkable, defying every expectation.

Perhaps the most profound moment came a few weeks after we

returned home. Mia, in her innocence, shared that she had a dream about Jesus during her ordeal. She said, **"He was with me,"** and that "He brought me home." Her words were a confirmation of what we had felt all along—that throughout this harrowing experience, Mia was not alone. Jesus was with her, comforting her, and ultimately, healing her. We were so excited to hear this, but we didn't want to stress her by asking a lot of questions and we didn't want to lead her in sharing what she experienced. I felt as if Jesus was confirming to me that His hand was on Mia.

The next time the topic of Jesus and heaven came up, we asked her, "What did Jesus look like?" She said very simply, "He looked a lot like God." Melissa later asked her, "What were you doing when you were with Jesus?" Mia replied, "He made me like an airplane." Melissa asked her, "How did He bring you back home?" Mia answered, "I don't know. He just did it with His hands, like magic."

A year and half later, Mia was with her brother and sister where she drew a picture of something. Mia held hers up for us, "Look daddy! This is the star I saw in heaven. It is really big and really bright." Later when I was alone with Mia I asked her, "Do you remember telling me about the star you saw in heaven? How do you know that there is a star in heaven?" Without any hesitation she looked at me and replied, "Because I was there." We have no doubt that she experienced something with Jesus. The best evidence for this is that she is still here.

Believing that God worked a miracle for our family does not take away from our gratitude for the many providers that cared for us during our crisis. We praise God fully, and we also appreciate the role these individuals played in our experience. We believed God used them in a huge way to keep Mia alive. We do believe that God could have stopped that tree branch in midair. However, working the miracle the way He did, the testimony has been witnessed by many and will have a greater Kingdom impact. He is sovereign and He will continue to work through the people who witnessed Mia's miracle.

Once home with time to process, Melissa wrote a letter to the EMTs who cared for Mia. Their office contacted us. They were so grateful for the letter and invited us to come as a family for a visit. We arrived surprised and so touched to see 40 to 50 people there to celebrate Mia. They made a slide show of the photos I sent to them. It was such a blessing!

Our gratitude extends beyond words—to the medical team, the community that prayed with us, and above all, to God for His mercy and grace. This experience has deepened our faith, taught us the true meaning of perseverance, and shown us the power of prayer. Mia's story is a testament to the fact that miracles do happen, and God's love and protection are real.

As we reflect on this journey, our message to others facing trials is to hold onto faith, to remember that even in the darkest moments, God is with us, guiding, comforting, and sometimes, performing miracles right before our eyes. Mia's life is a living testament to the power of divine intervention, a beacon of hope for anyone who hears her story.

In the end, our family's journey through this ordeal has brought us closer, made our faith unshakable, and filled our hearts with gratitude for every moment we have together. Mia's miracle is not just her story; it's a reminder for all of us that even in the deepest valleys, there is hope, there is light, and there is God's unfailing love.

FURTHER REFLECTION

The story of Mia's miraculous recovery reminds us that in our most desperate moments, God's presence is unwavering. When we face the impossible, our faith can be our anchor, guiding us through the storm. Reflect on the times when you have felt God's hand in your life, especially during trials. Trust that even when outcomes seem bleak, God is at work, orchestrating miracles and bringing comfort and hope.

PRAYER

Dear Lord,

Thank You for Your unwavering presence and the miracles You work in our lives. In times of fear and uncertainty, help us to trust in Your divine plan. Strengthen our faith, especially when we face trials that seem insurmountable. Grant us the perseverance to hold onto hope and the assurance that You are always with us, guiding and protecting us. May we always remember Your love and grace, finding peace in Your presence.

Amen.

CHAPTER 21

MIRACLES FROM A THEOLOGIAN AND PHILOSOPHER'S PERSPECTIVE

"Therefore I tell you, whatever you ask for in prayer, believe that you have received it, and it will be yours."
- Mark 11:24 (NIV)

Dr. JP Moreland is a renowned philosopher and a distinguished professor at Talbot School of Theology. He has taught theology and philosophy in several schools in the country and published a small library of works. He has been recognized as one of the top 50 most-influential living philosophers in the world. I was so honored to hear him share his book, A Simple Guide to Experience Miracles. In our time he was able to share a few of the vetted miracles in his book and some teaching around the supernatural and practical ways we can stir our faith and live supernaturally in Christ! - Julie

I am **Dr. JP Moreland**. My journey with miracles has been profound, involving firsthand experiences and encounters that have reshaped my understanding of the supernatural. A miracle, as I define it, is a supernatural intervention into the laws of nature for a purpose which changes things that happen. This includes not just God's actions, but also those of angels and demons, as the supernatural world interacts with us daily. Prayer, knowing God's Word and discernment are powerful tools given this reality of good and evil in the spiritual realm.

It is important to know the difference between a genuine miracle and a mere coincidence. This is important because in recognizing the miracles our faith is increased. Scientists have developed a principle to help differentiate between true miracle and coincidence. There are two factors in determining if an event was brought about intentionally for a purpose by an intelligent agent: (1) the event was a very improbable one, and (2) the event is capable of being identified as a special occurrence. The combination of those two things points to the intervention of an intelligent agent. This applies to an answered prayer.

One of the most remarkable cases I've witnessed is the healing miracle of Susan. Susan, a Jewish woman, was terminally ill with cancer that had spread to 51 points in her lymph nodes. After chemotherapy and radiation, her doctors had given up hope, and she was in hospice care. A friend from my church invited her to our Monday night prayer sessions. On her third visit, she felt a sensation like hot oil pouring from her head to her feet and intuitively sensed she was healed. Her oncologist confirmed this miraculous healing, showing no evidence that she ever had cancer. This led Susan to commit her life to Jesus, and she continues to live healthily today.

Prayer and healing have been central themes in my experiences. Effective prayer involves more than just asking; it requires a strong faith and understanding of the divine will. There are numerous reasons why prayers might go unanswered, such as timing, God's broader plan, or even demonic interference. However, these challenges should encourage us to persist in prayer and maintain our faith.

I have also encountered extraordinary international miracles. One compelling story involves a woman from Iran, a former thought police member. Disillusioned with Islam, she planned to kill her ill mother and herself live on a Christian TV show to denounce Christianity. The host, a former Lebanese Muslim who converted to Christianity, asked her on the air to pray to Jesus for a week. He agreed that if she did this and nothing happened that he would allow her to come back on the show in a week and allow her to follow through with her plan. She reluctantly agreed.

A week later the woman was waiting on the line to appear on the show. The show host was not sure what to expect but he put her on the show. "You won't believe this," she told him. "This week I noticed my mother up and walking and healed from her distended abdomen. I asked her what happened. She said that she prayed to Jesus and that Jesus appeared, put His hand on her stomach and healed her. He told her He wanted her to tell people about Him and what He had done for her." This miracle led not only to their conversion, but to numerous church plants!

People often ask why we don't see as many miracles in the West. One reason is our naturalistic worldview, influenced by science, which makes us skeptical of the supernatural. Additionally, people in the West rarely share their miraculous experiences due to fear of appearing foolish. I encourage sharing these stories to build faith within the community.

Near-death experiences (NDEs) provide further evidence of the supernatural. One well-documented case is Pam Reynolds, who underwent a novel and risky surgical procedure for a brain aneurysm. During the operation she was anesthetized, her body was cooled and drained of blood so they could work on the aneurysm. Her eyes were padded and covered. Her ears were plugged. She was effectively dead, with no brain activity. However, she later described in great detail the scene of the staff in the room, the surgical tools and conversations in the room, all of which were verified by the medical staff. She also reports that she met Jesus and He told her she would be alright but she had more work to do. Such evidential NDEs support the reality of the supernatural.

Living a supernatural life in Christ involves practical steps to increase faith. Reading the book of Acts is a great way to stir faith. Exposing oneself to credible miracle stories and reading reliable books on the subject can build faith. Engaging with others who have experienced miracles and practicing prayer regularly are also crucial.

FURTHER REFLECTION

Reflecting on Dr. JP Moreland's experiences, we see how the supernatural realm intersects with our daily lives, offering profound insights and miraculous interventions. Genuine miracles, distinguished from mere coincidences, bolster our faith and reveal God's active presence. The testimonies of healing, such as Susan's remarkable recovery and the transformative experience of the Iranian woman, underscore the power of prayer and the importance of unwavering faith.

Consider your own experiences and the moments when you've sensed a divine intervention or an inexplicable occurrence. How did these moments impact your faith? Take time to ponder the importance of discernment, prayer, and the recognition of miracles in your spiritual journey. Envision yourself seeking deeper understanding and greater awareness of God's miraculous work in your life.

PRAYER

Heavenly Father,

We thank You for the miraculous ways You reveal Your presence in our lives. Help us to discern and recognize Your hand at work, increasing our faith and trust in You. Strengthen our commitment to prayer, knowing that through it, we can experience Your transformative power. Guide us to share our testimonies, encouraging others to believe in Your boundless love and mercy. May our lives be a testament to Your miraculous interventions, bringing hope and inspiration to those around us.

Amen.

CHAPTER 22
A TRANSPLANT JOURNEY IN HEAVEN WITH JESUS

"Consider it pure joy, my brothers and sisters, whenever you face trials of many kinds, because you know that the testing of your faith produces perseverance. Let perseverance finish its work so that you may be mature and complete, not lacking anything."
- James 1:2-4 (NIV)

Pastor Mike was told he had two years to live. His diagnosis with a devastating lung disease has led to numerous surgeries and health struggles. Initially devastated, he ran to the Lord. Signs from God and an unimaginable encounter would bring revelation and call him to minister in new places. Even in his struggles, Mike chooses to keep a heavenly perspective and make every breath count. He loves sharing his testimony and the goodness of God with every chance he gets!
- Julie

I am **Mike Olsen**, and my journey truly began when I was diagnosed with idiopathic pulmonary fibrosis, a terminal lung disease, in 2014. However, to understand my story, we need to go back a bit. I was raised in a Catholic home and always knew about Jesus in my head but hadn't truly connected with Him in my heart. That changed when I was 19 and gave my heart to the Lord. This foundation of faith has been my anchor through all the challenges I faced.

In 2012, a severe ice storm hit Kentucky, cutting off our electricity for two weeks. My wife and I, along with our dogs, stayed warm by a wood stove, but the cold and the circumstances led me to develop pneumonia. This wasn't my first bout with respiratory issues; since moving to Kentucky, I'd been dealing with bronchitis regularly. After this episode, I visited an allergist who referred me to a pulmonologist. It was there that I received the devastating diagnosis: idiopathic pulmonary fibrosis. The doctor told me bluntly that this disease was worse than cancer and gave me two years to live.

Initially, I was shocked and devastated, but I turned to my faith. Instead of becoming bitter, I chose to get better. I ran to the Lord, seeking His word and guidance. In my chapel, I cried out to God, not asking why this was happening, but what He wanted me to do. I heard the words, **"Trust me,"** and from that moment, I felt a supernatural peace. Despite the grim prognosis, I decided to live my life to the fullest and use my experience to help others.

I began advocating for pulmonary fibrosis awareness, meeting with politicians, and even celebrities like Dennis Quaid, to bring attention to this disease. I was able to sing on stage with Dennis Quaid the song *A Whole Lot of Shaking Going On*. This is a bit comical because that was exactly what my life was like at the time (a lot of shaking). It was so much fun and I was able to touch a lot of people that night with my testimony. God even made a way for me to visit president Trump in the oval office to raise awareness of my disease. God opened doors that I would have never imagined. After my visit with the President, he signed into law the right for terminally ill patients to try medication that has yet been approved by the FDA.

I met many people, including a young man named Reuben from Texas, who was also struggling with pulmonary fibrosis. I learned that Reuben was planning to take his life the first night we spoke. Through late-night calls and encouragement, I helped him find a purpose, and he inspired me with his determination, participating in 5K runs with his oxygen tank. God used our exchange to encourage him. He fought a great fight before he lost his battle with pulmonary fibrosis. He went out of this world with a winning smile, a grateful heart and he made a difference with the time he was given. When we take time to listen to others God can use it power-fully. God used me at one of my lowest moments to minister to someone who was at an even lower place.

God rewarded me in my time of illness in other unexpected ways. Before I gave my life to ministry as a young man, I was trained in acting and dance in New York City. I loved it. When God called me to give it up I was sad to leave it, but I was obedient. During my time before the trans-plant, I was approached by a local news team and a newscaster Gilbert Corsey. He wanted to follow me for a year and create a documentary. *The Mike Olsen Story: I Am Dying Will You Help?* won an Emmy Award. 35 years after I gave up a career in acting I walked the red carpet to receive an Emmy. God has a sense of humor! He loves to bless us in unexpected ways.

Six months before I received my transplant, my wife and I experienced what we believed were divine signs. Friends were sharing things they felt God was putting on their hearts and echoed the exact words of my wife's private prayers. A friend told me I was going to experience some visions from God. One night, while driving home, a deer appeared on the high-way, and as we screamed out for help, "Jesus," it was like the deer disap-peared or we drove through it. This incident reminded us that God was aware of our struggle and that He had a plan for us.

So many people were telling me to claim healing, but God has His plan. His ways are higher than our ways. The Bible tells us to take up our cross and follow Jesus. A lot of Chrisitans don't want to talk about crosses. Nor do they want to talk about suffering. I like to refer to Hebrews 11 where it talks about suffering. There were many listed who were commended for their faith yet didn't receive what had been promised. Things don't always work out the way we plan or desire. It is about what God wants, what God ordains and what God says.

My journey took a miraculous turn when I had a heavenly encounter. Finally, in 2019, after five grueling years on the transplant list, I received the call for new lungs. The surgery was intense and lasted 12 hours. During the operation there was a problem with profuse bleeding and I had a near-death experience. I saw myself as I floated above the operating table and heard negative voices, which I rebuked in Jesus' name. As I ascended, I saw swirling, rainbow-colored lights and heard angels singing that I was coming home. But then, the Lord said I was just there for a visit.

In heaven, I was bathed in bright light as far as the eye could see. The glory of the Lord filled the heavenlies. The atmosphere was infused with molecules that were pulsating with the presence of Jesus. The very essence, His presence, His fragrance and His beauty permeated the whole atmosphere. As I stood in this place bathed with this light, I had an epiphany in heaven. I realized I couldn't remember my past. I couldn't remember any sin. It was like it had been erased from a blackboard. I felt so encouraged and blessed. I just felt, WOW... it was all Jesus! Everything we accomplish in life...it is all Him. All of the striving, all of the worrying! I realized I wasted SO much time worrying about finances, family, my spouse, how I appear to others, if I was doing enough, if I was pleasing God. It was like a weight had been lifted.

Suddenly I felt overcome with gratitude for my lung donor. My spirit cried out with thanks and I felt the presence of Jesus and my donor. I am not sure why, but I could not see the face of my donor clearly, but I knew with certainty who it was. The donor had their head lowered and I knew this was because he was so humbled to be called upon by Jesus. Jesus placed His hand on my shoulder and said, **"Mike, these are your new lungs. Receive them."** When I agreed, I was immediately brought back to my body. This experience assured me that my new lungs were a gift from heaven, and I felt a profound sense of peace and purpose.

The road to recovery wasn't easy. I was in a coma for ten days. I faced multiple complications and surgeries, but my faith remained steadfast. I also had angelic visitations, reminding me that God's presence was always with me. This journey taught me that we live in two realms-the earthly and the heavenly-and that Jesus is always orchestrating our lives.

Post-transplant, I continued to share my testimony, emphasizing the importance of organ donation. Despite the challenges, I remained grateful and focused on my mission to inspire and help others. Whether through my story or by making little prayer cloths shaped like lungs, I wanted to give back and make every breath count. My testimony is a testament to the power of Jesus, the reality of heaven, and the miraculous ways God works in our lives.

One of the most profound moments was when I felt the tangible presence of Jesus in heaven. In His presence, I felt completely free of guilt and sin, as if my entire past had been erased. This overwhelming sense of forgiveness and love was unlike anything I had ever experienced.

Living in the aftermath of such an experience, I feel a profound responsibility to carry the touch of heaven with me and to share the message of Jesus' love and power. My encounter with Jesus in heaven has deeply influenced my approach to life and ministry. It has taught me to let go of earthly worries and to trust in His divine plan, knowing that He is always in control.

My journey has been one of immense trials and miraculous triumphs. The suffering, the waiting for a transplant was tough. Although I didn't like it, none of it really matters in the light of eternity. The things that we go through might seem like they're gruesome and horrible down here, when in the light of eternity it is all woven into the fabric of who we will be. Through it all, my faith in Jesus has been my anchor. I encourage everyone to trust in the Lord, embrace every moment, and live with the assurance that heaven is real and Jesus' love is ever-present.

FURTHER REFLECTION

Mike Olsen's journey showcases the profound impact of unwavering faith and the miracles that can unfold even in the darkest times. His experiences highlight the importance of trusting in God's plan, even when faced with terminal illness and suffering. Mike's story is a powerful reminder that God's presence is with us, guiding and comforting us through life's challenges. His encounter with Jesus in heaven and the miraculous recovery post-transplant emphasize the reality of divine intervention and the importance of living with purpose and gratitude.

Reflect on your own life and the moments when you have felt God's presence, even in difficult circumstances. Consider how faith has been an anchor for you, guiding you through trials and tribulations. Think about the ways you can use your experiences to inspire and help others, just as Mike has done. Take a moment to meditate on the reality of heaven and the eternal perspective it brings to our earthly struggles.

PRAYER

Dear Lord,

We thank You for the miraculous ways You work in our lives, especially during our most challenging times. Help us to trust in Your divine plan and to find peace in Your presence. Strengthen our faith and use our experiences to inspire and uplift others. May we always be aware of Your guiding hand and live with a heart full of gratitude and purpose.

Amen.

CHAPTER 23
HOW MY FAITH HEALED ME FROM MULTIPLE SCLEROSIS

"But I will restore you to health and heal your wounds, declares the Lord."
- Jeremiah 30:17 (NIV)

Aurora was diagnosed with multiple sclerosis with four young children at home. She was told that her blindness was permanent and she would need a wheelchair. God would use her fraction of a mustard seed faith (as she admits) and her surrender to lead to a miraculous healing. He would train her to be a warrior on a path she would have never dreamed-51 triathlons, including three half Ironman! Today she is a stunningly beautiful woman filled with the love and light of Jesus! What an inspiration! - Julie

I am **Aurora Colello**. At 35, I was a stay-at-home mom with four kids under seven, living a seemingly normal life when I began experiencing severe pain in the back of my right eye. The pain escalated to the point where I couldn't move my eye without excruciating pain, eventually leading to complete blindness in that eye. The vision loss began as a squiggly line of blindness in the center of my eye, then progressed from that line down until one day I was completely blind in my right eye.

I was rushed for an MRI. The MRI revealed ten lesions on my brain and on my brainstem, and I was diagnosed with multiple sclerosis (MS). The neurologist informed me that my condition was incurable and progressive, predicting I would be in a wheelchair within five years. He said I would probably never get my vision back and that If I lived in a two-story home, I needed to consider moving to a one-story home because my diagnosis would move quickly.

The diagnosis was a devastating blow. My husband and I had just moved to California and were facing financial struggles due to the 2008 market crash. The news left me terrified about my future and my ability to care for my children. Desperate for answers, I began researching MS online, which only deepened my sense of hopelessness. Everything I read emphasized the incurable and progressive nature of the disease. My husband, a man of strong faith, encouraged me to turn to God. Initially, I was angry and confused, questioning why this was happening to me. However, his words prompted me to say a simple prayer, expressing my fear and placing my trust in God.

"God, I don't understand why You're doing this, but I'm going to trust You, and I'm scared to death."

This was a simple but honest prayer that I prayed with the smallest fraction of a mustard seed of faith. At that moment I felt a shift. It was as if God took me by the hand and led me on this journey. Everything changed after surrendering it to God. I began to pray about the next steps. God led me to learn about options. In a bid for more information, I sent out an email to everyone I knew, seeking others with MS. The responses I received were varied, with most people sharing negative experiences with conventional medications. However, one response mentioned a holistic center near me that taught dietary changes and supplements for managing MS and other diagnoses.

Skeptical but desperate, I visited a functional medicine doctor at a holistic center. The holistic approach seemed unconventional, focusing on diet, supplements, and cranial massages to stimulate the optic nerve. Honestly, I initially thought they were crazy for telling me I needed a neck massage, but the doctor told me that the nerves of the eye connect to the neck and this would help stimulate my sight to come back. Despite my doubts, I followed their protocol strictly. Remarkably, within days, I began seeing flashes of light and color in my blind eye.

When I shared my progress with my neurologist, he dismissed it as the nerve firing without any real recovery. They said I would never get my vision back and I should not hold on to hope. Despite his skepticism, I knew something significant was happening. I decided to completely follow whatever my functional medicine doctor advised. Miraculously, within two weeks of following the holistic plan of care, my vision was back better than it was before I went blind. I wore contact lenses and was due for a checkup during the time I was blind, so I had to reschedule. When I went in after my vision came back, my ophthalmologist said that she had to decrease the prescription in my right eye because my vision had improved. This was the same eye that I have been blind in for over 30 days!

At this point I was all in with holistic, unconventional and functional medicine and focusing on my lifestyle, correcting deficiencies, reducing inflammation, and managing stress. I kept getting stronger and seeing improvements. My medical doctors were angry with me for not listening to them, but God was giving me such an undeniable peace about which path to take. I do believe there is a place for traditional doctors and traditional medicine, but God was not leading me there at this time. It was the first time I felt what the Bible refers to in Philippians (4:7) where God gives us a peace that surpasses all understanding, even in the scariest of circumstances.

During my healing journey I was encouraging a friend who signed up for a triathlon. She challenged me to join her. I was not an athlete. I didn't even own tennis shoes. Interestingly, God brought to my mind a memory that had been imprinted in my mind from many years prior when I was volunteering at the Ironman in Kona. I remembered seeing and cheering on a woman who was hobbling across the finish line late in the race. I came to run alongside her for encouragement. When we came into the finish area I was able to see her cross the line in spite of her pain and hear announced on the loudspeaker, "Congratulations, Sarah, you are an Ironman!" The crowd was showering her with applause as she finished her race. As a young woman, I had never experienced such inspiration. I was in awe.

Although I had never done anything athletic, I decided to do one sprint triathlon. There was still a small thought in the back of my mind that remembered what the doctors said about the wheelchair. In case they were right, I wanted to accomplish what I could while I was still able. The training and discipline of being an athlete was new for me. We set training goals to prepare and I feel God was giving me something to not just keep my focus off of my disease, but He was training me to fight my battle. He was creating a warrior. God used it to train my brain, my spirit and my body to be strong. As I made progress, God was breaking my limiting beliefs.

People began to hear about my diagnosis and I began to see the athletic arena as a platform to share my faith and my story of fighting MS. The first triathlon was such a great experience for me that I continued to train and race. Although I was feeling well, it was time to do another scan to check the lesions in my brain. I found a wonderful ayurvedic neurologist who ordered a follow-up MRI. A year into my journey, after multiple scans without improvement, she was amazed to share the news with me that my scans were clear of any lesions. There was no sign of demyelination! This miraculous recovery was beyond conventional medical explanations and affirmed my decision to trust in holistic methods guided by faith.

Following my healing, I was inspired to pursue more athletic challenges. I continued to get stronger. I have been so blessed to participate in over 51 triathlons, including, half Ironmans, and using my platform to share my story. My healing journey has been featured in magazines and in interviews.

Throughout my journey, I faced significant challenges from the medical community. Many neurologists dismissed my holistic approach, with one even terminating me as a patient. However, the undeniable evidence of my healing in the form of multiple MRIs kept me grounded in my belief in God's guidance.

My story has reached people worldwide, offering hope and inspiration to many. I have spoken at conferences, shared my experiences in interviews, and helped others through personal consultations. I decided to study functional medicine, getting the education behind my story and how I healed my body, and I continue to share my knowledge and support those who reach out to me and need help guiding them to healing through functional medicine.

To anyone facing a similar struggle, I would say there is always hope in Christ. Even when you don't see it, He is working! Trusting in God and taking actionable steps toward healing, whether through dietary changes, lifestyle adjustments, or seeking the right support, can lead to incredible outcomes. My journey has shown me the power of faith and the importance of addressing all aspects of health—physical, mental, emotional and spiritual. My miraculous healing journey serves as a testament to the power of faith, perseverance, and holistic approaches to health.

FURTHER REFLECTION

Aurora Colello's journey from despair to miraculous healing offers profound lessons on faith, resilience, and the holistic approach to health. Despite a devastating diagnosis and a bleak prognosis, her story highlights the transformative power of trusting God and seeking unconventional paths to healing. Aurora's strict adherence to a holistic regimen, combined with unwavering faith, led to her remarkable recovery and new purpose in life.

Reflect on the moments when you've faced seemingly insurmountable challenges. How did your faith guide you through those times? Consider the importance of being open to different approaches and the role of a supportive community in your healing journey. Ponder the significance of holistic well-being—addressing not just the physical, but also the mental and spiritual aspects of health.

PRAYER

Dear God,

Thank You for the miracles You work in our lives, even when circumstances seem dire. Help us to trust in Your plan and seek guidance in every aspect of our lives. Strengthen our faith, especially in times of trial, and open our hearts to the support and wisdom around us. May we find hope in Your presence and courage to pursue paths that lead to healing and wholeness.

Amen.

CHAPTER 24

I WAS SAVED BY TWO ANGELS AFTER A LOGGING TRUCK ACCIDENT

"For he will command his angels concerning you
to guard you in all your ways."
- Psalm 91:11 (NIV)

Bruce miraculously survived an unimaginable trauma and is a witness to God's healing power and angelic protection. His testimony includes a verifiable out-of-body experience, angels and the spiritual realm, divine promptings, a medically documented creative healing miracle and more. His personal journey is one that includes tremendous periods of suffering but also redemption. God has called him to ministry where Bruce continues to witness miracles. He is faithful, obedient while giving God the glory! Amazing! -Julie

I'm **Bruce Van Natta**, and I want to share my incredible journey with you. It's a story marked by a miraculous encounter where I was saved by angels.

Growing up, I didn't have a strong religious background. My family rarely attended church, perhaps only on Christmas and Easter. Despite my parents believing in God, our home was filled with dysfunction. Yet, God had a different plan for me, drawing me closer to Him in the years leading up to November 2006.

In the year before the accident, my wife and I started participating in Bible studies and small groups at our house. I was working on a book about hearing God's voice, unaware of how crucial this would become. Two months before the accident, I finished the book. Little did I know, I would soon be crying out to God and experiencing His voice in a profound way.

On November 14th, I was working on a logging truck. My wife had pleaded with me not to go to work, believing we were being disobedient to God's call for us to enter full-time ministry. I was frustrated and resistant, slamming my fist on the table in anger. Just two days later, her fears came true.

I was at a remote logging camp, finishing up repairs on a logging truck. The engine was running, and I was wiping off my tools when the other mechanic, Leonard, asked me to look at one more thing. Reluctantly, I agreed. My steel frame creeper (rolling device we use to slide under a vehicle) was packed and, luckily, I decided to use the one in the shop. Lying on Leonards' plastic frame creeper under the truck, I was unaware that the jack holding up the truck was unstable. Suddenly, I saw movement out of the corner of my eye. I turned just in time to see the jack slip. In an instant, the truck's axle, which has five to 6 tons of weight on it, came crashing down on my midsection with an unimaginable force. The sound of this was similar to a loud explosion as the truck hit the concrete.

The pain was beyond description. It felt like my entire midsection had been flattened. Blood shot out of my mouth from the internal injuries, and I realized the severity of my situation. Instinctively, I called out, "Oh Lord, help me. Lord, help me." Fortunately the plastic framed creeper collapsed, allowing a small space for my body. On the left side of my body there was approximately one inch of air space between the concrete and the axle. On the right side there were a couple inches of air space from the concrete to the axle because the driver-side wheel was still on the truck.

Leonard, in shock, was paralyzed momentarily. The loud noise of the truck crashing down had drawn his attention, and he turned to see the horrifying sight of my crushed body. He quickly snapped out of it and dialed 911, screaming for help. Leonard was able to jack the truck up enough that I could see my flattened body. My immediate thought was that my body looked cartoonish. My next thought was that there is no way a human body can survive such a trauma. I was terrified the jack was going to slip again. Suddenly, after the truck was lifted I felt incredibly weak and it was getting hard to breathe.

As I lay there, something extraordinary happened. I felt my spirit leave my body. It was as if I was floating, hovering 14-16 feet near the ceiling of the garage. From this vantage point, I saw everything clearly—the chaotic scene below, Leonard's frantic movements, and an injured man broken and bleeding beneath the massive truck. Oddly, I was completely disconnected from my physical body. I didn't realize the man under the truck was me.

A profound sense of peace enveloped me, unlike anything I had ever felt. Despite the trauma below, up there, I felt no pain, no fear, only tranquility. I saw the volunteer paramedics arriving. I could hear the conversations in the room. Even though I could see the chaos, I didn't feel scared or nervous. I noticed Leonard at the front of the truck on his knees crying, running his hand through the injured man's hair. He was saying that it should have been him under the truck. I heard a few people say it was too late for the man under the truck. I heard them call for a helicopter. Somehow I heard all of this at once, yet I felt perfect peace.

It was then that I noticed two enormous angels on either side of my body. They appeared to be eight feet tall. These angels were emanating a bright, comforting light. They had long hair and wore robes with belts. I did not see wings. They were very muscular and focused. Their hands were positioned over my lower abdomen, the worst part of my injuries. Oddly, this seemed very normal to me to see them. They were there, silently present, as witnesses and protectors in my time of dire need.

I watched as the first responders arrived, each taking in the scene with a mix of urgency and despair. All of the EMS responders entered the garage from the main entrance. I noticed the last two, a gray-haired older man and red-headed young woman, entered through the back doors. The red-haired woman was named Shannon. Despite others on the scene declaring me dead, Shannon refused to give up. She knelt by my side and began praying fervently, "Bruce Van Natta, come back."

Her voice cut through the chaos, familiar and powerful. Each time she called my name, I felt my spirit being pulled back toward my body. As I was pulled back into my body, I instantly had the painful realization that it was me under the truck. The pain was indescribable and I was unable to see the angels while in my body. Three times, I left my body and was drawn back by her prayers. The second and third time I left my body, I saw a very long tunnel opening up at approximately a 45-degree angle with bright light at the end. I knew without any doubt that Jesus was at the other end of that tunnel. I went into the tunnel and I was moving so fast that I felt a g-force. I feel I am nearly halfway into the tunnel and I hear someone calling my name.

Each time, I was faced with an overwhelming choice: give up and die, or fight to live. As I hovered between life and death, I could hear two distinct voices. There was a loud voice that was telling me to give up and die. I know now that was the enemy. Yet, there was a still small whisper offering life, despite the pain and the daunting road ahead. God was telling me if I wanted to live that it was going to be a hard fight. God knew I was going to spend the next year of my life in the hospital. He knew I would have to learn to read and write again, learn how to walk again. He knew there would be many days in my hospital room that I would beg God to let me die.

In those moments, Shannon's prayers grew louder, more desperate. "Sir, you are on the verge of life and death. What do you have to fight for? Do you have a wife? Do you have kids?" Their faces flashed in my mind. Her words struck a chord deep within me, and I found a renewed will to live. I knew immediately that it was the Holy Spirit speaking through her. The thought of leaving my loved ones behind gave me the strength to endure the unbearable pain and the grueling battle that lay ahead.

Finally, with a surge of determination, I chose to fight. My spirit reentered my body, and my heart started beating again. The pain was excruciating, but I was alive. I was airlifted to our state's biggest trauma center. They operated on me for hours. The head surgeon told my family that in all his years he had never seen anyone this traumatized make it to the

I WAS SAVED BY TWO ANGELS AFTER A LOGGING TRUCK ACCIDENT

hospital alive. He said he didn't expect me to live through the hour. My wife and our friends prayed and gave thanks to God for every 30 minutes of life.

The journey to recovery would be long and taxing with multiple surgeries and an induced coma. There was extensive damage to my spine, my intestines, major arteries and internal organs. I knew I had to fight for my family, for those who loved me, and for the life God had given me. There were times I was angry with God.

I do remember waking up for the first time in the hospital and desperately wanting to tell my family that I saw angels. I still had a breathing tube so I could not speak. I was unable to write the word down and it left me so frustrated. It felt like forever before I was able to share my news with my wife and brother and a nurse. **"ANGELS! I saw these two huge angels!! God sent these angels!"** That was all I could talk about.

One of the most amazing miracles God worked was in the healing of my intestines, which is documented in my medical records. At one point I was left with an amount of intestine that is not compatible with life. This is documented several times in my medical records. I had to be fed intravenously for months and my weight dropped by 65 pounds. My own aunt didn't recognize me. The doctors said they could only keep me alive for a matter of months. God then wakes up a man in New York two mornings in a row and tells him to fly to Wisconsin and pray for me, that He is going to do a miracle. I was on their church's prayer list. He flies to my hospital room, lays his palm on my forehead and prays and commands my small intestine to grow back in the name of Jesus. I was not familiar with this type of prayer. I can tell you it felt like electricity moved from his hand into my body and it felt like a hose or snake uncoiled in my belly.

Soon my weight starts to climb. The doctors were unsure what was happening. They had to adjust my parental nutrition. Eventually they decided to do a barium test and that is when they saw 9-11 feet of my intestine! Surgical records and pathology records all reflect that I was left with less than 100 cm of intestine. My last big operation for some clean up with my gallbladder and rib was an open operation. When the same surgeon who had removed my intestine saw the 9-11 feet of intestine return, he turned and threw the scalpel across the room and had a melt-

163

down. He was an atheist, a medical genius who couldn't reconcile what he was seeing. When he was later interviewed, he admitted that when he witnessed this case that he knew a higher power was involved.

About a year after my accident I went to thank the EMS workers that helped save my life. I arrived at their monthly meeting to see many of those who were at the scene. I pointed out eight people who I saw from the ceiling. When I saw Shannon and the older gray-haired man, I asked them why they came in the wrong door. Initially they had forgotten, but then they remembered that they missed the main driveway and drove up a secondary driveway. Shannon, the red headed woman who prayed me back to life three times, was a two-month-old baby Christian. She had moved into a new home and they were experiencing paranormal activity. This revelation of a spiritual realm led her to seek help and ultimately to accept Jesus.

As I reflect back on my prayer at the scene of the accident, **"Lord, help me."** I think about the baby Christian, Shannon, who prayed, I think about the angels God sent. I think about God waking up a man and telling him to pray for a healing of my intestines and I am overwhelmed with gratitude. Each of these pieces were pivotal in my survival. They were a testament to God's power and His plan for me, even in the face of seemingly insurmountable odds. This experience reinforced my faith and set me on a path to share my story, to testify to the miracles I had witnessed, and to spread the message of hope and divine intervention.

Today, I share my testimony through Sweet Bread Ministries, reaching out to schools, churches, jails, and anyone willing to listen. My story is not about me but about God's mercy and grace. It's a testament to His power to perform miracles and His love for us, despite our flaws.

I encourage anyone listening to this story to open their hearts to God. No matter how broken you feel, He hears you and loves you. If you're struggling, remember that God's grace is sufficient, and His power is made perfect in our weakness. I'm living proof of His miracles, and I'm here to share that hope with you.

FURTHER REFLECTION

Bruce Van Natta's testimony powerfully illustrates the reality of divine intervention and the presence of angels in our lives. His miraculous survival and recovery demonstrate God's ability to work through seemingly impossible circumstances. Bruce's story encourages us to trust in God's plan, even when we face overwhelming challenges and feel on the brink of despair. His experience serves as a reminder of the importance of faith, prayer, and the assurance that God hears our cries for help.

Reflect on moments in your life when you have felt God's presence, especially in times of crisis. Consider the ways in which faith and prayer have provided strength and comfort. How can you remain open to the possibility of miracles and divine intervention in your own journey? Ponder the significance of sharing your experiences to inspire and uplift others.

PRAYER

Lord,

Thank You for the miraculous ways You reveal Your power and presence in our lives. Help us to trust in Your plan, even when we face insurmountable challenges. Strengthen our faith and remind us that You are always near, ready to help and guide us. May we find comfort in Your presence and the courage to share our stories to inspire hope in others.

Amen.

CHAPTER 25

GOD LEADS AN ENTREPRENEUR TO DO THE UNIMAGINABLE

"For what profit is it to a man if he gains the whole world, and loses his own soul?
Or what will a man give in exchange for his soul?"
- Matthew 16:26 (NKJV)

Imagine if God led you to a level of financial success that you never dreamed was possible, only to prompt you to walk away at its peak performance? Randy shared how God blessed him with a successful chain of video rental stores and how He clearly led him to exit. His obedience was the difference between losing everything or retiring with financial freedom at age 36. Making the decision he did afforded him time and resources to provide and care for loved ones and gave him the blessing of teaching others about money management from a godly perspective. He has been blessed to see many of his students excel from what they have learned in his teaching. God continues to work through Randy. - Julie

My name is **Randy Halcomb**, and I'm from Alabama. My upbringing was strict; my dad, a former Marine, ran our household, most of the time, like the Marines. At the age of 16, seeking something different, I ventured to a Christian boarding school in Oneida, Kentucky. Right after high school, lacking funds for college, I joined the army for the G.I. bill, which eventually brought me to Fort Rucker, Alabama. That's where my life started to take shape in ways I could have never predicted.

I met my future wife, Darlene, in a small town not far from the base. She came from a very poor tenant-farmers family, the youngest of seven kids. Neither one of us had any money, but we were in love. There was just something about her, I knew she was the one. Wouldn't it be great if it worked that way for everyone? Nine months from the night we met, we got married. I got out of the Army, and we went to college to become schoolteachers. We became missionaries and went back to Kentucky, but soon returned to Alabama due to Darlene's parents' failing health. I found work as a seventh-grade computer teacher.

One day, the school's librarian approached me about a broken VCR, knowing I was a little tech-savvy. VCRs were very expensive back then, a new technology, and she was desperate to get the schools only VCR repaired. She said she couldn't find anyone, anywhere to fix it. Curiosity got the best of me, and I dismantled the VCR on my kitchen table, in our modest trailer home. Discovering the issue was a minor, easily replaceable part, I fixed it for just fifty cents. This sparked an idea. I placed a small ad in the newspaper: "VCR Repairs." Calls started flooding in. Before I knew it, my trailer was overflowing with VCRs needing repairs. I was making more money repairing VCRs than teaching school with a college degree. My wife, bless her heart, tolerated the chaos. This sideline job, eventually led us to open a small VCR repair shop.

We were making lots of money, more than we had ever dreamed, and thus decided to venture into video rentals, offering movies at just 99 cents. It was a huge success. We expanded, opening more stores, and even ventured into building shopping centers to house them. Life was great! Money was abundant. We lived by Christian values, always closed on

Sundays, but our focus was slowly shifting. Now, we didn't rent X-rated movies, just all the hardest R-rated movies that the public wanted.

Then one day my life took a sudden turn. I had a really bad toothache and went to my dentist, a devout Christian, who told me reluctantly, **"God told me to tell you this... Many of the movies you rent in your video stores don't come from God."** That hit me hard. It was like a wake-up call I didn't know I needed. I brushed it off initially, rationalizing our success and charitable acts, but deep down, I knew something had to change.

The very next day, a young boy came into one of our stores asking for a horror movie, "Freddy Krueger, mommy," he wanted. His mother told him that he'd already seen that movie four times. That moment, coupled with the dentist's warning, was like a one-two punch to my conscience. Not long after, I received a letter from a little girl who said she was a local third grader, and wanted to know, as a Christian, how we could rent some of the movies we were renting. It was becoming clear; I was profiting from something that totally conflicted with my biblical faith and principles.

I began to question all that I was doing. The turning point was a scripture that came to me, while I was talking to the bank president; "What does it profit a man to gain the whole world and lose his soul?" That's when I knew I had to make a change. I prayed, seeking guidance for selling the business. The conditions I laid out in prayer were specific, almost impossible: a buyer who would retain all my employees, take over the leases, and match my investment that I had made in the past nine years. I calculated the exact amount I had invested into the business and kept it on a piece of paper.

God answered in the most unexpected way. One day, out of the blue, a man from a large video chain walked into one of our stores and said, "We want to buy you out." I took out the piece of paper with the amount I had invested. The offer he made matched, to the dollar, the figure I'd prayed for and written down. It was a clear sign. Selling wasn't just a financial decision; it was a test of faith, a commitment to living according to God's will. Six months after selling our chain of stores, the entire industry went to DVDs. If I hadn't listened to God, we would have lost it all.

After selling, I returned to teaching, this time in college, focusing on entrepreneurship and biblical money management. This part of my journey was about more than just making money; it was about using God-given resources wisely, making ethical decisions, and helping others to do the same.

Presently, my days are filled with teaching Bible classes at our church, a role that brings me immense joy and fulfillment. My life is full, enriched by the presence of my grandchildren and the responsibility of caring for my aging parents. It's a testament to the journey God has led me on, from a young entrepreneur to a steward of His Word, teaching and living by the principles that have shaped my life.

My story isn't just about a successful business venture; it's a testament to faith, ethical dilemmas, and the power of prayer. It's about recognizing that success isn't measured by wealth or status but by how closely we align our lives with God's Word. To anyone facing moral or ethical cross-roads, my advice is to pray specifically, listen for God's guidance, and trust that His plans for us are always greater than our own ambitions.

FURTHER REFLECTION

Randy Halcomb's journey reminds us of the profound impact of aligning our actions with our faith. His story highlights the importance of integrity and listening to God's guidance, even when it challenges our worldly success. Randy's decision to sell his video rental business, despite its prof-itability, demonstrates the power of faith and the necessity of living in accordance with biblical principles. His testimony encourages us to seek God's will in all areas of our lives and to trust in His plans.

Consider the moments in your life when you faced ethical dilemmas or challenging decisions. Reflect on how your faith has guided you through these times. Are there areas in your life where you need to seek God's guidance more earnestly? Take time to pray for clarity and the courage to make choices that honor your faith and values.

PRAYER

Lord,

Thank You for the wisdom and guidance You provide in our lives. Help us to seek Your will in all that we do and to make decisions that align with Your principles. Give us the courage to act with integrity, even when it is difficult. May our lives reflect our faith and bring glory to Your name. Guide us to use the resources and opportunities You provide wisely and ethically.

Amen.

CHAPTER 26
HOW JESUS RESCUED ME FROM THE DEMONIC

"For our struggle is not against flesh and blood, but against the rulers, against the authorities, against the powers of this dark world and, against the spiritual forces of evil in the heavenly realms."

- Ephesians 6:12 (NIV)

Melissa had great intentions in her New Age practices and a good heart but was naive to the dangers of the spirit realm. Her low point was marked by a vivid vision of what demons planned to do to her in hell. Nonetheless, the enemy's plans were no match for the powerful prayers of her mother. I love this testimony of deliverance and how God is now working through Melissa with giftings for the Kingdom of God! - Julie

I am **Melissa Hendricks**. Before I was even born, my mother's appendix burst. The doctors advised her to abort me, but thankfully, she didn't. I was born healthy. My early years were marked by a miraculous event. At the age of four, I got a mosquito bite that led to a rare disease. No one had survived this disease, and I was being treated at the University of

Minnesota. My grandmother prayed fervently for me, and I believe it was the Lord who healed me because there was no medical cure for that disease. This early brush with death and recovery was the first indication of a greater spiritual journey ahead.

Growing up, I felt a strong pull toward the New Age and occult practices. Even as a child, I was fascinated by books on palm reading and other esoteric subjects. I thought these interests were normal, assuming everyone could see the colors, words, and images in the spirit as I did. It was only later that I realized these experiences were unique and significant, marking the beginning of a deep spiritual conflict in my life. I believed all practices led to God. I studied and experimented with anything spiritual, convinced that it would bring me enlightenment and fulfillment, but it gradually led me down a darker path. I began reading tarot cards and conducting readings for others, often getting paid for my services. Over time, I stopped using the cards and started channeling directly, believing that I was communicating with a higher power. I thought I was being used by God, not realizing that I was being deceived by the enemy.

During this time, my mother had a profound spiritual awakening. She became a Spirit-filled Christian and started praying earnestly for me. She kept a prayer journal, recording scriptures and prayers for my deliverance. One of her favorite scriptures was Isaiah 49:25 (NKJV), which says, **"But thus says the Lord: Even the captives of the mighty shall be taken away, and the prey of the terrible will be delivered; for I will contend with him who contends with you, and I will save your children."** She prayed that I would come home for Christmas, despite not knowing where I lived at that time.

My mother's prayers were powerful, and they began to work in ways I didn't immediately understand. Despite being fully immersed in the occult, I started to become curious about the Bible and Jesus. I got a hold of the Bible and read the books of Job and Revelation, interpreting them through a New Age lens. However, I started to question how Jesus fit into all of this. Many in the New Age movement saw Him as a great teacher or prophet, but I began to wonder if there was more to His story.

As I explored deeper, I decided to ask Jesus to help me. This decision triggered a massive spiritual attack. I experienced physical manifestations of spiritual battles, including snakebites that appeared on my skin. The malevolent spirits that I had once thought were my guides and protectors now revealed their true nature. They were not benevolent at all. Instead, they were dark and evil, bent on tormenting and destroying me. I was shown a vision that was as clear as a movie projected on a wall. The spirits showed me what they intended to do to me in hell. I saw myself being tortured in a place that looked like a nightmarish torture chamber. The demons around me were laughing and mocking, taking pleasure in my fear and pain. They showed me in excruciating detail how they would tear me apart and torment me for eternity.

This vision was not just a threat; it was a stark, horrifying reality that they wanted to instill in me. It was a clear message: if I continued on the path I was on, this would be my fate. The fear and the darkness that surrounded me were overwhelming. I felt myself sinking deeper into despair, unable to escape the grip of these evil forces.

In my desperation, I consumed all the drugs I had in my possession, hoping to numb the pain and escape the relentless spiritual attacks. I then went to a friend's house, looking for some semblance of safety. However, my erratic and paranoid behavior only frightened my friends. I was trying to explain the spiritual attacks I was experiencing, but my words sounded incoherent and unbelievable. They thought I had lost my mind and called an ambulance.

The medical staff, seeing my distressed state, called my parents. My parents picked me up the next day, which was Christmas Eve-the exact day my mother had been praying for my return. My mother, who had been fervently praying for my salvation, believed that this was a sign that God was answering her prayers. I asked my mother if she could take me to church. Despite the spiritual turmoil and confusion, something within me longed for the peace and understanding that I had been seeking.

At the church service, they invited anyone who needed prayer to go to the back of the sanctuary. I went, still reeling from my recent experiences, and met a kind woman who explained the concept of salvation to me. She asked if I wanted to receive Jesus into my heart, and I said yes. She then led me in a prayer, and as I accepted Jesus as my Savior, I felt an overwhelming sense of peace wash over me. It was as if a heavy burden had been lifted from my shoulders. I also received the baptism of the Holy Spirit, which was a profound and transformative experience.

At that moment, I was supernaturally delivered from my addictions to alcohol and drugs. The cravings and the hold these substances had on me were completely gone. It was a miraculous deliverance that I could only attribute to the power of God. This experience marked the beginning of a new chapter in my life, one that was centered on my relationship with Jesus and my newfound faith.

After my conversion, I entered a period of intense spiritual growth. I refer to this time as "Bible boot camp." I attended church services twice a week, joined two prayer groups, and went to a healing school to learn about physical, mental, and spiritual healing. This rigorous spiritual regimen helped me understand my identity in Christ and how to pray for deliverance and healing.

My mother showed me her prayer journals, which contained detailed records of her prayers for me, including specific information about my life that only God could have revealed to her. This reaffirmed the power of prayer and God's personal care for me. I moved out, got a job, and continued to immerse myself in spiritual growth. The Lord emphasized patience, teaching me that deliverance and healing are processes that happen in His timing.

Twenty-six years have passed since my conversion, and the Lord has peeled away many layers of my old life. He has taught me to teach others about spiritual warfare, deliverance, and the power of prayer. I continue to pursue Him, desiring to glorify Him through my testimony. My journey from the New Age and occult to a committed Christian life has been marked by significant spiritual battles and miraculous deliverance. Through prayer, perseverance, and the grace of God, I have found true peace and purpose. My testimony is a testament to the power of prayer and the transformative power of Jesus Christ.

FURTHER REFLECTION

Melissa Hendricks' journey from the occult to a committed Christian life underscores the profound power of prayer and the transformative grace of Jesus Christ. Her story reveals the dangers of New Age practices and the deceptive nature of evil spirits. Through the unwavering prayers of her mother and her own desperate cry for help, Melissa experienced a miraculous deliverance that led her to a deep and genuine relationship with Christ.

Reflect on areas of your life where you may be seeking fulfillment or answers outside of God's will. Consider the importance of prayer and how it can bring about powerful changes, even in the most dire circumstances. Think about the people who have prayed for you and the impact their prayers have had on your life. How can you deepen your own prayer life and trust in God's timing for deliverance and healing?

PRAYER

Lord,

Thank You for Your transformative power and the gift of prayer. Help us to seek You in all things and to trust in Your plans for our lives. Deliver us from any deception and lead us into Your truth. Strengthen our faith and guide us in our journey toward spiritual growth and healing. May we always rely on Your grace and share the hope we have found in You with others.

Amen.

CHAPTER 27
A FORENSICS EXPERT RECEIVES PROOF OF GOD

"'For I know the plans I have for you,' declares the Lord, 'plans to prosper you and not to harm you, plans to give you hope and a future.'"
- Jeremiah 29:11 (NIV)

Randy's life revolved around physical evidence. He was a homicide detective and an expert in blood spatter interpretation for over 30 years. In March 2020 his life changed when diagnosed with COVID and in a coma for 22 days with a 3 percent chance of survival. His testimony includes a physical healing miracle as well as supernatural encounters. Randy feels confident God has given him more than enough evidence to know that He is not just real and active, but strategic. To see Randy's face light up as he shared his newfound revelation about a very real and present God has brought so much joy and encouragement to so many people! Just amazing! - Julie

I am **Randy Schiefer,** and my life story is intertwined with my professional career and deeply personal experiences. From a young age, I faced significant losses that shaped my life and career choices. My father died suddenly of a heart attack when I was just 16. I was so very close to my father. He was a reserve deputy sheriff, and this intrigued me. We were on a vacation when he collapsed. My mother was frantic as I tried desperately to resuscitate him. This event had a profound effect on me. It was an event that left me with deep guilt and a lasting fear of death. This fear was compounded when my sister died of stomach cancer at 38, a traumatic experience that further influenced my professional path.

Growing up, my family wasn't particularly religious. We attended church sporadically, and God was not a central part of our lives. This lack of religious foundation made me skeptical of spiritual matters. My career in law enforcement, especially as a homicide detective, reinforced my need for tangible evidence. I relied on physical evidence to solve cases, and this mindset made it difficult for me to accept anything without concrete proof. There was circumstantial evidence at church, but not enough to convince me that God, the afterlife and heaven were real.

In 1972, I joined the Air Force and started working as a security police officer and eventually transitioned to the office of special investigations. My work involved advanced training in death investigation, and I became an expert in blood spatter interpretation. I attended numerous autopsies and dealt with death regularly, which was both professionally challenging and personally numbing. Reflecting on my work, I believe I brought many families resolve in their loss, which may in some way have linked to meeting the need for my own resolve in the tragic losses of my past.

In March 2020, my life took an unexpected turn when I was diagnosed with COVID-19. What began as a joke about the virus quickly escalated into a life-threatening situation. I was hospitalized with bilateral pneumonia, and within days, I was intubated and placed on an ECMO machine with multiple-organ failure with bleeding disorders. My condition was critical, and my family was told I had only a 3 percent chance of survival.

I went into a 22-day coma, I had several near-death experiences (NDEs) that profoundly changed my perception of life and death. These experiences were vivid, detailed, and left a lasting impact on me. During this time I experienced hallucinations and dreams, but I also had times where I felt very much alive and I traveled.

In one of my NDEs, I found myself in a beautiful golden city with magnificent skyscrapers and lush green parks. The streets were immaculate, exuding a sense of peace and tranquility. Despite the beauty, I felt lost and alone, unable to see anyone else.

Eventually, I encountered someone with brown hair and a beard, wearing a dark robe. He confirmed the city's beauty but told me I didn't belong there and directed me toward large oak doors. I passed through the doors, still feeling lost, and wandered through the city until I found a pristine white staircase. As I began to climb, I heard a voice saying, "There he is, there's Randy, get him." I felt someone grab me, pulling me back to my dark, sedated world.

Another occasion that I found myself back in this heavenly city there appeared a very animated young boy. He had a bowl-shaped haircut, olive skin and shorts and was barefoot. "Follow me!" he said with excitement. He took me into another room. It was beautiful. It had these big, round, pedestal chairs throughout, and a big picture window. He asked me to wait and he ran off. I remember looking through the picture window and seeing a river that ran under the building. It was lined with the same beautiful flowers and trees. There were people near the bank of the river just relaxing. As I am taking in this gorgeous view, the little boy comes back and says, "I'm sorry. You have to leave. Your room is not ready." Suddenly, I was back in darkness.

During another NDE, I awoke in a dimly lit void, aware of my death. As I moved through the darkness of the void, my deceased mother-in-law and brother-in-law suddenly appeared. My mother-in-law had passed away from Lou Gehrig's disease, which had ravaged her body and mind. In my vision, she appeared youthful and healthy, probably in her mid-30s. She had her hair pulled up into a bun with a white ribbon and wore a white robe. She sat very regally, exuding peace and serenity, a stark contrast to the suffering she endured in life. I was overcome with emotion and began calling out to her, "Dolores, Dolores, it's me, Randy!" But she did not acknowledge me. Instead, she looked away, which puzzled and saddened me deeply. My deceased father, mother, and sister appeared, standing deeper in the void, but I definitely sensed some kind of barrier that was separating me from my family.

As I stood calling to my family, an orb of light appeared rapidly, stopping inches from my face. Instantly I saw a human face. The face conveyed an urgent message: **"Tell Madison at the salon her grandfather's okay."** He moved on to a white porch. On the porch I saw him with red, white and blue ribbons and American flags. Somehow I knew he was a Veteran. I then found myself back in the hospital bed, remembering the message vividly.

My daughters, especially my youngest, who is a nurse, played a crucial role in advocating for my treatment. They fought tirelessly to get me convalescent plasma, despite initial resistance from the hospital. Their efforts, combined with a widespread prayer chain over 45 states and five countries, resulted in a miraculous recovery. During a pandemic, so many people volunteered to travel and help donate. It brings me to tears to think of all of the strangers that prayed and volunteered and cared about me during this time. I will never forget their kindness.

Special authorization had to be made with the blood bank for the plasma. There was a local pastor who was a match. I received the plasma on Good Friday. On Easter Sunday morning, just days after receiving the convalescent plasma, my organs began to heal, and I regained full function without any lasting damage. The ECMO was off. My kidneys and liver healed that week. I did have to learn to walk again, to swallow again, but my organs are healthy.

After waking from my coma, I felt a strong compulsion to find Madison and deliver the message. I had no idea who Madison was, but I felt responsible to fulfill this task. Upon returning home, I found a business card for a local barbershop in my dresser, which mentioned Madison Logan. My daughter, Lisa, made an appointment with Madison for me. I had no recall of who she was or how I obtained the card.

At the barbershop, Madison confirmed that her grandfather, a veteran in Iowa, had passed away. I delivered the message from my NDE, which deeply moved her. Madison confirmed that her grandfather John's home in Iowa had a white porch and that he loved sitting on the porch. Every Veterans Day, Madison and her family would help John make red, white, and blue ribbons for the veteran graves, a detail I couldn't have known. As I sat in her salon chair we were both in happy tears and in awe with the confirmation of this message and the connection to this man. The card in my dresser is a mystery to me, but God's hand is clearly visible.

This encounter comforted Madison and reinforced my belief in God's plan. I later found out that there were other parallels between Madison's grandfather John and myself. We are both veterans. Interestingly, John died suddenly of a heart attack and Madison's younger sister tried to save him but was unable. This brought me back to the memory of losing my father to the heart attack and the guilt I carried with it. I was given an opportunity to bring comfort to a family that had suffered as I did.

I have become friends with this family in Iowa and plan to visit the very white porch I saw in the vision of John. Later they were able to show me photos of John at different ages and it matched the exact face that I remembered from the vision. God gave me more proof!

I no longer fear death. I have no doubt there is a God and an afterlife. I carried guilt and trauma for over fifty years but it no longer plagues me. I have found a place of healing where I have fully released the guilt. I want to encourage others who are suffering with guilt and trauma that healing is possible.

I am now committed to sharing my story and these experiences to help others understand that there is a purpose behind even the most extraordinary circumstances. I am so grateful to be alive today. I know I am only here now through the grace of God. I didn't deserve another chance, but He gave me one. I thank Him daily. Through my testimony, I hope to bring comfort to those who fear death and to those grieving the loss of loved ones. God's plan is intricate and often beyond our immediate understanding, but it is always purposeful, guiding us toward deeper faith and connection.

FURTHER REFLECTION

Randy Schiefer's experiences demonstrate the profound impact of near-death experiences (NDEs) and the ways they can transform our understanding of life and death. His story highlights the reality of spiritual encounters and the importance of faith in navigating life's most challenging moments. Randy's journey from skepticism to a deeper belief in

God's plan underscores the significance of trusting in divine guidance and the power of prayer.

Reflect on your own perceptions of life and death. Consider how faith influences your understanding of these profound experiences. Think about the ways you can seek and recognize God's presence in your life, especially during times of fear and uncertainty. Ponder the significance of spiritual encounters and how they can offer comfort and direction in your journey.

PRAYER

Lord,

We thank You for the profound ways You reveal Yourself to us, even in the darkest times. Help us to trust in Your plan and to seek Your guidance in every aspect of our lives. Strengthen our faith and open our hearts to Your presence. May we find comfort in knowing that You are always with us, guiding us through life's challenges. Use our experiences to bring hope and understanding to others.

Amen.

CHAPTER 28
JESUS SHOWS A MAN IN HEAVEN THE CRUCIFIXION

"This then is the message which we have heard of him, and declare unto you, that God is light, and in him is no darkness at all."
- 1 John 1:5 (NLT)

Wayne suffered a heart attack just seven days after he accepted Jesus as his Savior. He was blessed with a profound time with Jesus in a near-death experience. Miraculously Wayne did get to the hospital after his incident to confirm a heart attack, however there was no residual damage to his heart muscle! Wayne is a lawyer from Texas who is currently working in Australia. He has also worked as a contractor in military defense. His near-death experience has left him with a voracious hunger for reading scripture and he is passionate in sharing that Jesus is real and that His love for each one of us is more than we can fathom. - Julie

I am **Wayne Fowler**. When I opened my eyes, I realized I wasn't in bed anymore. Instead, I was standing beside my bed, looking down at my own body. It was an odd sight, seeing myself lying there, lifeless, with my hand clutched to my chest and a painful expression frozen on my face. My vision, though, was incredibly sharp, far beyond what my glasses ever allowed me to see. I could make out even the tiniest details around the room.

As I looked around, I noticed my wife was still sound asleep. Then, I heard a voice calling my name from behind me, "Wayne." I turned around to see who it was, and I found myself looking out through the wall and the window as if they weren't even there. Outside, sitting on the curb, was a woman named Linda. Although I didn't recognize her from my life, there was a deep, internal knowing that I knew her.

I walked out through the wall toward her. Linda was bathed in a circle of light, like a spotlight from above. She greeted me and told me that someone wanted to meet me. As I looked up in the direction she indicated, I saw a distant point of light in the sky. Suddenly, I felt large, unseen hands lift me up. It was like being a child picked up by a parent, warm and reassuring.

I began to rise, leaving Linda behind as I ascended toward the light. My body glowed with a bluish-purple light, and I could see through my hands and feet as if they were made of translucent light. I noticed that I was wearing clothes and shoes, which struck me as odd since I had been in bed.

As I ascended, I saw the landmasses of Earth recede below me, and I entered a tunnel that opened up before me. This tunnel was dark, but around its edges were angels, packed shoulder to shoulder, creating a welcoming procession. They were excitedly talking among themselves, celebrating my arrival.

The speed of my ascent increased, and I realized I was moving faster than the speed of light. This initially made me uncomfortable, but as soon as I thought about it, I slowed down just enough to feel comfortable. I continued toward the light at the end of the tunnel, which grew larger and brighter as I approached.

Bursting out of the tunnel, I entered a realm filled with light. And in this realm of light was another light that outshined them all. This light was brighter than ten thousand suns, but didn't hurt my eyes. It was stunningly beautiful, pure and alive. As I looked closer, I saw the form of a man in the center of this light, with light pouring out from Him.

As I got closer, I could make out the form of a man in the center of this light. His arms were outstretched as if welcoming me into a loving embrace. I could see that the light was emanating from Him. **This was Jesus! This is God! This is the Way, the Truth, and the Life!** The moment I recognized Him, I knew without a doubt that He was the creator of every-thing. The love that flowed from Him to me was overwhelming. It filled me completely, making me feel as if I could explode from its intensity.

Entering the light was like becoming part of it. It entered me just as I entered it, filling every part of my being with a profound sense of love and knowledge. This love was beyond anything I had ever experienced on Earth. It was pure, infinite, and unconditional. Words like rapture, bliss, and ecstasy barely begin to describe it. It was as if all the joy and love in the world were concentrated into a single moment, and then multiplied infinitely.

As I stood there, enveloped in this love, I began to ask Jesus questions. Each question was answered instantly and completely, with a depth of knowledge that was beyond comprehension. It was as if He could antici-pate every possible follow-up question and answer it all at once. The answers were not just words, but complete volumes of understanding, filling my mind with knowledge.

One of the most profound moments was when I was taken to the very place and time of His crucifixion. I was there, standing before Jesus as He hung on the cross. I could feel His thoughts, His pain, and His love. I under-stood in that moment that he would have gone through all of that just for me, even if I were the only person in all of creation to accept Him. This real-ization brought me to my knees. The love and sacrifice were overwhelming. I knew that this love of Jesus applies to each and every one of us. He would have endured the cross for each and every one of us. This left me in awe.

I continued to ask questions, and Jesus continued to answer. Each answer brought more understanding and more love. I learned that every-thing about Him and the Bible is true. The more I learned, the more I real-ized how much there was to know. It was like being a child again, filled with curiosity and wonder, asking my father endless questions and receiving answers that were beyond anything I could have imagined.

During this time, I also felt the presence of the Father. Although I couldn't see Him, I knew He was there. I could hear Him and interact with Him. His presence was powerful and loving, just like Jesus. This place felt more real and more like home, more than any place on Earth ever had. It was like returning from a long journey and finally being where I belonged.

Despite the overwhelming love and knowledge, I realized I couldn't stay. When I asked if I could remain there, both the Father and Jesus firmly said no. Their voices were powerful yet loving, leaving no room for argument. I understood that I had to return to Earth. The realization was disappointing, but I knew it was necessary.

As I was pulled back through the tunnel, I saw the angels again, still celebrating my journey. The speed of my descent was just as fast as my ascent, and I passed through the layers of the atmosphere, seeing the Earth from space. It was a beautiful sight, a reminder of the world I was returning to.

I re-entered my house, passing through the roof and ceiling, noticing every detail along the way. I re-entered my body with such force that it rebounded off the end of the bed and landed face down in the middle of the floor, waking my wife, Denise. In the darkness of the night, she was startled and confused, and I was very weak. Summoning all of my strength, I turned my body and crawled to the edge of the bed reaching out to her to catch her attention. With a worried voice she said, "Wayne?!" With one last burst of energy, I managed to squeak out, **"I just...met...God!"**

This experience changed my life in ways I could never have imagined. It affirmed my faith and gave me a deeper understanding of the love and truth of Jesus. I now share my testimony with hopes to inspire and bless others with my story-with His story.

In conclusion, my encounter with Jesus was a profound and transformative experience. The love and knowledge I received were beyond anything I had ever known. I am grateful for the opportunity to share my story and pray that it brings others closer to understanding the love and truth of Jesus.

FURTHER REFLECTION

Wayne Fowler's experience offers a profound glimpse into the reality of Jesus' love and the eternal truth of His existence. His encounter with Jesus in a realm of indescribable light and love provides a powerful reminder of the depth of God's love for each of us. Wayne's journey emphasizes the importance of faith and the transformative power of divine encounters. It reassures us that Jesus' love is unconditional and His presence is always with us.

Reflect on the moments in your life when you have felt God's presence or experienced His love. Consider how these experiences have shaped your faith and understanding of God's nature. Ponder the significance of knowing that Jesus' love is personal and infinite, and how this truth can influence your daily life and interactions with others.

PRAYER

Lord,

Thank You for the overwhelming love and truth You reveal to us. Help us to embrace Your presence and live in the light of Your love. Strengthen our faith and deepen our understanding of Your divine nature. Guide us to share Your love and truth with others, bringing hope and inspiration to those around us. May we always seek to draw closer to You and live in a way that reflects Your infinite love.

Amen.

CHAPTER 29
JESUS HEALS A MAN OF TERMINAL CANCER

"My flesh and my heart may fail,
but God is the strength of my heart and my portion forever."
- Psalm 73:26 (NKJV)

There aren't many people that radiate the love of Jesus quite like Chuck Keels. Being filled with this love was a process that involved hardship. Cancer once ravaged Chuck's body. He was given no hope and referred to hospice. God had another plan. An encounter with Jesus in the hospital became a launching pad for a new life and calling. Truly one of the most inspiring and loving people I have met, he is passionate in serving and equipping others to live FULLY through his Living Hope Cancer Foundation! - Julie

My name is **Chuck Keels.** I grew up in a big family with two sisters and three brothers in Ohio. I loved my small town and working on a farm and being outside. We were active in our church, and I attended a Christian school for 11 years. While I knew the Bible stories well, there was always a sense that something was missing in my life. Despite my faith, I felt a spiritual emptiness that I couldn't quite identify. I believed in God and Jesus, but my relationship with Him wasn't personal.

As I got older, I became a single dad to my two boys. We moved around a lot, living in Arizona, California, Ohio, and then back to Arizona. Looking back, I realize I was dragging my boys all over the country because I was lost, searching for something beyond this world. Despite achieving financial success, I still felt off track. I had a substantial bank account, a beautiful home, and could take my kids on vacations, but none of it brought the happiness I was looking for.

In 2015, I began experiencing unusual aches and pains that I couldn't ignore. As a healthy guy who always went to the gym, these symptoms were alarming. Despite the increasing discomfort, I brushed it off, assuming it would pass. But the pain got worse, and eventually, I couldn't ignore it any longer. On a Friday night, after taking my boys out to eat, I decided to go to the emergency room to find out what was wrong. At the hospital in Gilbert, Arizona, they ran scans and tests. The first result came back quickly—a computer-generated x-ray showed that I had two fractured vertebrae. This was shocking because I hadn't fallen or injured myself. The doctor said it wasn't uncommon, but they needed more scans to get a complete picture.

At 2 AM, the doctor came into my room, shut the curtain, and sat down next to me. She looked at me and said, "Chuck, I have bad news. Everything you're experiencing is cancer-related." This was the first time I heard the word "cancer" in relation to myself. My head started spinning. They planned to bring in a specialist the next day to do biopsies and determine the extent of the cancer.

After the biopsies, I went home to wait for the results. Over the next three days, my condition worsened. The pain was excruciating, I was losing weight rapidly, and my hair was thinning. They had put me on the highest level of liquid morphine for the pain. When I returned to the doctor, he looked at me in disbelief and said, "I can't believe you walked in here. Your scans show cancer in 90 percent of the bones in your body. It started in your prostate and has spread everywhere. You're in stage four, and you might have three months to live."

Hearing this was devastating. I had to prepare for the end, for the sake of my boys. I was placed in hospice care, taken out of medical care, and given a hospital bed for my home. My body was breaking down rapidly, and I couldn't climb the stairs anymore. We planned to move back to Ohio so my family could take care of my boys after I was gone. We bought plane tickets, and I started giving away everything I owned because moving all our possessions across the country didn't make sense when I had only three months to live. Strong faith was not part of my journey at this time but I had so many people praying for me.

Our last night in Phoenix, we stayed at a resort near the airport. That morning, as I walked down the hall, something in my back popped, and I collapsed in excruciating pain. I couldn't move or breathe properly. Hotel security and the fire department arrived, and eight guys managed to get me onto a stretcher and into an ambulance. Every bump on the way to the hospital sent sharp pain through my body. They took me to John C. Lincoln Hospital, where they ran more scans and tests. The doctors decided to operate in hopes of buying me more time and alleviating the pain.

During my stay at the hospital, something miraculous happened. While in recovery, the doctors came and explained that the surgeries went perfectly. I was soon to be transferred out of the recovery room. I was alert and observing the nurses and activity in the room. Suddenly, I felt the room turn frigid cold. I looked around, trying to figure out where the cold air was coming from. When I turned back, I saw a figure standing next to me, I thought it was a doctor. However, he was wearing a brown robe and a white scarf. I found this peculiar. As he reached out and touched my shoulder, I heard a voice in my head that said I was in the presence of Jesus. It was a brief encounter, but the impact was profound.

I was stunned and confused by what had just happened. I didn't know Jesus well, but I knew this encounter was real. When the nurses came to check on me and asked about my pain level, I told them I didn't feel any pain. They were puzzled, considering my recent surgery and broken back. From that moment on, I never needed another pain medication.

That night, unable to sleep, I had a deep conversation with God. Still confused about what had transpired, my condition momentarily improved, yet still a death sentence looming. I thought about my kids without a father. I cried out to God, "God, what gives?!" I asked Him why I was going through this and what His plan was for me. I heard a clear message: **"You've been a fighter your whole life. What are you doing?...As long as you're alive, be fully alive."** I immediately sat up on the side of the bed and decided to go wash my face and to stop feeling sorry for myself.

I got out of bed, walked two laps around the hospital floor without pain, and felt an overwhelming sense of gratitude. I thanked God for the relief and the chance to live again. Despite being exhausted, I felt a renewed sense of purpose. I promised God that whatever He was going to do in my life that I was 100 percent in. The next morning, I was determined to live fully. This conversation with God at age 50 was the first time I had established a personal relationship with Jesus.

After ten days in the hospital, I was discharged and moved to the Mayo Clinic for three weeks. My mindset had completely changed. I was ready to fight and knew I had been given a second chance. I started chemotherapy and began to regain my strength. I started talking to God regularly and began hearing his voice in my thoughts. Despite the grueling treatments, I felt better every day. I was determined to live my life fully and help others do the same.

The physical progress I made was unusual. The chemo was meant to try to extend my life a bit, but I truly believe that when Jesus touched me in the hospital that I was cured of every cancer cell and broken bone in my body. I didn't know it at the time. In month three of chemo I got a scan with my very skilled doctor. She entered the office smiling ear to ear, "I couldn't wait to see you today! I have studied cancer all over the world and I have never seen anything like this in my career. Your journey is not of medicine. It is miraculous! Your scans are like those of a normal healthy guy."

Even more amazing, the doctor sent me for a bone scan to check my bone density. They couldn't believe the results and said if they hadn't seen me in the first round that they wouldn't believe the scans were from the same person. My bones were perfectly clean. The miracle was undeniable. Soon I began to get calls from people asking what they can do to fight cancer.

During this time, I met a beautiful young lady named Hannah, who also had stage-four cancer. We shared a deep faith and a commitment to living fully despite our diagnoses. Hannah and I fell in love and got married. We started the Living Hope Cancer Foundation together to help others navigate their cancer journeys. Our foundation provides support, guidance, and resources to cancer patients and their families, focusing on prayer, love, nutrition, and physical activity.

Our foundation grew rapidly, reaching people worldwide. We wrote books about our experiences, sharing our stories to inspire and guide others. We created videos and other resources to help cancer patients and their families. Despite the challenges, we found joy in our mission and in each other.

Tragically, Hannah's body couldn't handle the treatments, and she passed away on November 29. It was the hardest thing I've ever experienced, but I found peace knowing she was with Jesus, free from pain and suffering. I continue to honor her legacy through our foundation, helping others and spreading the message of hope and faith.

Today, I am committed to Living Hope Cancer Foundation and its mission. I travel, speak at events, and share my testimony to inspire others. My journey has taught me the importance of faith, love, and living fully. Despite the hardships, I am grateful for the blessings and the chance to help others through their toughest times.

Living with cancer is not easy, but through faith and support, we can find hope and strength. My story is one of miraculous healing and profound transformation, and I hope it inspires others to find their own paths to peace and joy.

FURTHER REFLECTION

Chuck Keels' journey from despair to miraculous healing exemplifies the profound impact of faith and divine intervention. His encounter with Jesus transformed his life, giving him a renewed sense of purpose and determination to live fully. Chuck's story highlights the importance of turning to God in our darkest moments and trusting in His plan, even when faced with seemingly insurmountable challenges.

Reflect on the times in your life when you have felt lost or in need of a miracle. Consider how your faith has guided you through those moments and brought you closer to God. Ponder the significance of living fully and embracing the life that God has given you, regardless of the circumstances. How can you use your experiences to inspire and help others in their journeys?

PRAYER

Lord,

Thank You for the miraculous ways You work in our lives and for the gift of renewed purpose. Help us to trust in Your plan and to turn to You in times of need. Strengthen our faith and give us the courage to live fully, embracing the life You have given us. Guide us to use our experiences to inspire and support others, bringing hope and faith to those around us.

Amen.

CHAPTER 30
AN ATHEIST IS RADICALLY TRANSFORMED BY SUPERNATURAL EXPERIENCE

"The LORD is my shepherd; I shall not want. He restores my soul; He
leads me in the paths of righteousness For His name's sake."
- Psalm 23:1,3 (NKJV)

Darin was an atheist at odds with his faith-filled wife. He accused
her of chasing the invisible man. Their marriage was on the rocks when
their precious two-year-old son was near death after a severe case of
croup. During this tragic time, God moved in a supernatural way,
which led to a radical transformation in Darin and brought comfort to a
family facing loss. Darin became captivated by the Bible, the only thing
that could give him language for what he had experienced. Other blessings include a saved marriage and a new spiritual gifting! - Julie

I am **Darin Hamm**. Our story begins with the challenges my wife
Jennifer and I faced early in our marriage. We disagreed on matters of
faith. Despite our love, we were often at odds, making our home life difficult. We had a son, Griffin, whose birth was a blessing but added to our
stress as first-time parents. During this time our marriage was struggling.

My wife's Christian counselor even advised her to leave the marriage. Our situation seemed to worsen when Griffin, previously a healthy child, suddenly fell ill with croup.

After multiple visits to doctors and assurances that Griffin would recover, we ended up in the emergency room. His condition deteriorated rapidly, leading to cardiac arrest. Despite the efforts of the medical team, Griffin was declared brain-dead. In those heart-wrenching moments, we were given a final 24 hours with him. Jennifer spent eight hours lying beside him, and then it was my turn. She wanted me to have time with him. Initially it was so difficult for me. I just couldn't accept what was happening to our son.

As I lay down with Griffin, the room darkened, and I was engulfed in an overwhelming sense of despair. It hit me that I never taught my son how to do a proper handshake. I reached out to grab his little hand and touched his head with my other hand. The moment I touched his head, I found myself in a completely different realm. This was not a vision. I felt physically present in a different place. Everything was a beautiful, vibrant blue, and Griffin was with me, more alive than ever. He held my hand and led me forward at an incredible speed, yet without any sensation of wind. Griffin was ecstatic, looking at me with joy and love. However, every time he looked away, I felt an unbearable emptiness. Griffin and I were able to know one another's thoughts.

During this time, I became acutely aware of God's presence. The love and truth of God were overwhelming. I was completely mesmerized at how much I was loved. I was taught deep, absolute truths about life, love, and my purpose. I even experienced a life review, where I saw my actions and their impacts from God's perspective. This included seeing how I had mistreated an employee, realizing my duty to love and care for others as God loves us. I realized that the good things I thought I had accomplished in my own strength were actually the doing of Jesus. I was blown away by this! I saw how He protected me when my life was in danger. Truly amazing!

At the endpoint of our journey, Griffin, filled with excitement, communicated to me that he was seeing Jesus. Although I couldn't see Jesus, I felt His presence profoundly. Griffin then asked me if he could stay. My response wasn't a simple yes or no. It was beyond a yes. I expressed a deep realization of the afterlife, God's love, and the ultimate purpose of life, which is to be with Jesus. This "wow" encompassed all these realizations and was beyond a simple affirmation. I knew he was in the best possible place imaginable. I couldn't bear to say no.

Instantaneously, I was back in the hospital room, holding Griffin's hand. The darkness was gone, replaced with an overwhelming peace and sense of transformation. I was a changed man. It was a night and day change. This profound experience filled me with a new purpose and an insatiable desire to learn about God. The following day, I bought a Bible and began to immerse myself in scripture, understanding my experience through the word of God. The Bible was so alive to me. It helped me have language for what I experienced.

My transformation was evident to everyone around me, especially my family, who saw a complete change in my demeanor and outlook. Jennifer, too, noticed the change and, although she struggled with her grief, found solace in my transformation. She shared how a Christian counselor advised her to focus on the blessings in her life, which significantly helped her cope with the loss.

Three years later, I had another profound experience during my father's illness. He was a strong, loving man who had accepted Jesus into his life. When he suffered a major heart attack, I refused to leave my father's bedside, holding his hand. I felt led to pray the 23rd Psalm over him. I prayed this prayer for one hour and forty-five minutes, the whole time they were working to revive my dad. After what felt like an eternity, the lead doctor approached us. She was compassionate but firm, explaining that my father had been without sufficient oxygen for far too long. She said it was time to let him go, as he was likely brain-dead and would never regain consciousness. I understood her words, but my heart refused to accept them. I kept praying.

"The Lord is my shepherd, I shall not be in want. He restores my soul. He guides me in paths of righteousness for his name's sake."

Suddenly, something extraordinary happened. As I prayed, my father regained consciousness, looked at me and was moving his hands trying to get out of bed. I looked at him and I screamed, "Dad! You died! Were you with Jesus?!" He clearly nodded yes. Shocked, I called Jennifer back into the room. The lead doctor, witnessing this, was astounded. She had been convinced my father was beyond saving, yet here he was, responding to us. He went to surgery after this but ultimately passed from complications. We felt blessed to have had that last exchange with him and to know that he was with Jesus.

These experiences have led Jennifer and me to dedicate our lives to helping others. We have shared our testimony widely, offering hope and faith to those in despair. I have specifically been led to reach out to individuals struggling with suicidal thoughts, sharing the reality of the afterlife and God's love, helping them find a new purpose in life.

Our journey has been one of profound transformation, faith, and love. We have seen the incredible power of God at work in our lives and the lives of those around us. We hope our story brings hope and faith to others facing similar struggles.

FURTHER REFLECTION

Darin Hamm's story underscores the profound power of faith and the transformative impact of divine encounters. His journey from despair to a deep, personal relationship with God highlights the importance of seeking God's presence and trusting in His plan. Darin's experiences with his son Griffin and later with his father reveal the reality of God's love and the afterlife, offering hope and purpose even in the darkest moments.

Reflect on the times in your life when you have faced overwhelming challenges. How has your faith guided you through these experiences? Consider how God's love and presence have provided comfort and direction. Ponder the significance of these divine encounters and how they have shaped your understanding of life's purpose and the reality of the afterlife. How can you use your experiences to inspire and support others in their faith journey?

PRAYER

Lord,

Thank You for Your profound love and the transformative power of Your presence. Help us to trust in Your plan, even in the midst of our greatest challenges. Strengthen our faith and guide us to seek You in all things. May we find comfort in Your love and use our experiences to inspire and support others. Teach us to live with purpose and to share the hope and faith that You have given us.

Amen.

CHAPTER 31

COMFORTING SIGNS AFTER
THE LOSS OF A SON

"Blessed are those who mourn, for they will be comforted."
- Matthew 5:4 (NIV)

In July of 2016, Hudson Adams was 19 and working at a Christian summer camp doing what he loved the most: teaching kids about Jesus. Tragically, he became ill and passed away from primary amoebic meningoencephalitis caused by an amoeba known as naegleria fowleri, an organism that affects the brain. His family and community were heartbroken with the loss of such an outstanding young man. Even in a time of tragic loss, God provided miracle after miracle of comfort, reassuring that Jesus is real and has Hudson wrapped in his arms. The level of faith that his father has displayed during such a crucible has left an indelible impression on me. Surely the faith of Job! - Julie

I am **Stephen Adams**. My testimony begins in a hospital, a place where I experienced one of the greatest shocks of my life: the passing of my son, Hudson. When Hudson passed away, I was in complete disbelief. I walked out of the ICU, overwhelmed and searching for answers. I encountered one of Hudson's mentors, Phil, and in my state of shock, I desperately asked him if Hudson was okay. Phil's simple nod gave me a glimmer of reassurance, but my mind was filled with two pressing questions: Is Hudson truly gone, and if God is real, is Hudson okay in eternity?

Hudson went into the hospital on a late Monday night. By Tuesday morning, we knew he was going to pass away. The doctor confirmed our worst fears, and that afternoon, we faced the heart-wrenching task of telling Hudson's 10-year-old sister that he was going to pass away. It was incredibly hard to see her struggle with the finality of the situation, repeatedly asking if it was 100 percent certain.

During this painful time, our friend Diane had an experience that provided us with immense comfort. While Diane was alone visiting Hudson in the ICU, she suddenly could see him looking beautiful and fully restored. At the foot of Hudson's bed, she saw Jesus holding him. Diane told us about this experience months later when we were more able to process it. This experience reassured us that Hudson was in Jesus' arms, bringing us a sense of peace amidst our grief. To think that the God of the universe was holding our son was so personal and comforting.

Less than a day after Hudson passed, my daughter contacted a stranger over social media who had lost a child. Our family had heard about her loss. My daughter messaged her and expressed she was worried about us and if she would talk to us. This woman, a stranger, told us that God had already told her to come and talk to us. That in itself revealed that God was moving on our behalf. She came to our home that morning and helped us to see that everyone grieves differently and we have to allow each other freedom to grieve in our own way. God speaks to us all in our own unique way. This helped us to have grace in our family as we all did grieve differently.

There were many signs and encounters that further comforted us. One of my wife's friends, in a rush to get to the memorial service, wanted to get a necklace engraved with Hudson's name. At a jewelry store, she was shown a selection of necklaces that had been returned, and the first one she saw was already engraved with "Hudson." My wife wears that necklace as a cherished reminder. There were countless other instances where Hudson's name appeared in unexpected places, which felt so comforting.

Another significant moment was when Hudson's little sister told my wife that Hudson had visited her. She was surprised and asked him if he was real. He said yes. She said she felt him just like she could feel her mom's arm, providing a tangible sense of his presence and reassurance that he was okay. My older daughter also had a dream where Hudson told her he was okay, which ended precisely as her alarm went off, making the message feel even more profound.

Personally, I had a dream where Hudson flew a small float plane and landed it on a beautiful, crystal-clear lake. He ran to me, hugged me, and told me he loved me. He then said, "Dad, I am learning so much." This dream felt different from any other and gave me a sense of peace, as if Hudson was communicating directly to me. Flying was always a dream of his. This felt like such a blessing from God. I felt God was showing me that he is not resting in peace, but he is fully active and learning.

One of the most profound reassurances came through the song "Swing Low Sweet Chariot." This song held special meaning as it was the only one I remembered my dad singing to me, and I sang it to all my children, including Hudson. The day we buried Hudson, our neighbor encouraged us to be open to signs from God. That very day, at church, they sang "Swing Low Sweet Chariot" twice, which had never happened before. Subsequently, the song continued to come up unexpectedly and meaningfully, including a priest in Jerusalem who was not aware of our situation, insisting on singing it with a friend of mine on the anniversary of Hudson's death. I felt God was telling me that He had Hudson, enveloping him in His love.

A week after Hudson's passing, my wife found a book by Dietrich Bonhoeffer, a theologian Hudson admired. She handed it to our daughter, who landed on a page discussing death and eternal life. Bonhoeffer's words about life triumphing over death through Jesus Christ felt like a direct message from God, reassuring us of Hudson's eternal life.

When tragedy strikes it is tempting to ask and focus on the question, "why?" I have learned that trying to figure out the why is never going to bring peace. Seek the presence of God. He will show up and comfort you. He is faithful. Even so, with the miracles and signs being such blessings in our time of grief and loss, we are grateful for them, but we keep our eyes on Christ.

Frontier Camp played a crucial role in Hudson's life. It provided him with a spiritual mentor and friends who shared his faith. The camp community supported us immensely after Hudson's passing, but more importantly, it had helped shape Hudson into a young man whose teacher described him as "Christ at our school."

Reflecting on Hudson, he was always smiling, kind, and concerned for others. He would come home from school, often crying about a classmate in need and asking how we could help them. He was known for his kindness and always had a smile on his face. Every child who has been lost has had a purpose and value.

Sharing my story has been a way to honor Hudson's memory and the impact he had on those around him. It's also a testament to how God has wrapped His arms around us, providing reassurance through countless signs and the unwavering presence of His love.

A spiritual truth that Hudson was passionate about sharing at camp:

Everybody is saved by grace through Jesus Christ and there is nothing else you have to do other than accept that gift to get into heaven.

- Hudson Adams (Ephesians 2:8-9)

FURTHER REFLECTION

Stephen Adams' story illustrates the profound impact of faith and the comforting presence of God during times of immense grief and loss. The experiences shared by Stephen and his family reveal how God's love and reassurance can manifest through dreams, signs, and the supportive presence of others. These divine encounters provide a deep sense of peace and remind us of the eternal life promised through Jesus Christ.

Reflect on the moments in your life when you have faced significant loss or hardship. How has your faith helped you navigate these challenges? Consider the ways God has shown His presence and provided comfort during these times. Ponder the importance of remaining open to

His signs and the reassurance that comes from knowing our loved ones are in His care.

PRAYER

Lord,

Thank You for Your comforting presence and the signs of Your love during our times of grief and loss. Help us to seek Your presence and find peace in Your promises. Strengthen our faith and guide us to remain open to Your reassurances. May we find comfort in knowing our loved ones are with You and continue to share the hope and faith we have found in You with others.

Amen.

CHAPTER 32
A DYING MAN SEES JESUS BEFORE PASSING

"Jesus said to her, 'I am the resurrection and the life. The one who believes in me will live, even though they die.'"
- John 11:25 (NIV)

Chaplain David Carl was a young man when he heard the audible call of God for his life. He has witnessed the supernatural in his 45 years of service. It was an honor to meet with him and hear about his experiences. His work has blessed countless individuals! Thank you, Chaplain Carl! - Julie

I am **Chaplain David Carl**. Hospice chaplains tell me that every one of us will have a death vision when we die. This term is used to describe the experience of seeing deceased loved ones shortly before you pass away. Not all of us will have a chance to talk about these visions, but I've been with a person who had that chance.

I got a call to see someone in the oncology unit. This gentleman is suffering with cancer that has metastasized. He is a skeleton of himself. As I remember, he was in his late 70s. He was exhibiting breathing patterns of someone in their last breaths. I was called with hopes of offering support for him and his large family at the bedside.

He's getting close to the end of life. He is semi-conscious. His eyes are closed. He's breathing hard. You can hear a little bit of what we call the death rattle, which means death is near. His extremities are cold. All the symptoms the nurse shared with me were true. Eight family members are lovingly at his bedside caring for him. I am encouraging them.

I addressed the family, "This is a wonderful time to share your stories with him, your appreciation for him, what you loved about him. If there's anything you need to forgive him for, this is a great time to do that. If there is anything you need to ask forgiveness for, this is a great time. This is a sacred time. He can still hear you. His eyes are closed. I know he's breathing hard, but he's still with us."

As I was sharing this, all of a sudden this frail, semi-conscious patient sits straight up in a bolt-like fashion. He's staring at the wall in front of him. One family member jumped up to get the nurse in fear that he was in pain. "Hold on a second. Let me check with him," I offered. I said, "Mr. Smith, it's Chaplain Carl here at the request of your family. I can't help but notice your eyes are wide open. You're looking at that wall. Do you see anything?" He nodded yes.

"Could you tell me what you're seeing?" I asked. He started naming about six to eight different family members who had died, some of whose names the family in the room did not know. They were witnessing this reunion of sorts, a welcoming party.

And then he exclaims, "Oh my gosh! Wait a minute… Who's that?" And he said, **"Oh, WOW! Could that be? I…I think that's Jesus!"** He has this air of contentment about him. Everyone is watching, many are crying their eyes out, some speechless and awestruck. I don't know how I found the words, but I asked, "What's Jesus saying?" He replies, **"Welcome home!"** He reclined back in his bed. Within a matter of minutes, he was dead.

There were lots of conversions in that room. People sometimes wonder, is my loved one going to heaven? Or are they going someplace else? All those answers got squared away right now. And people who were in the room, they started talking about the different relatives and experiencing their loved one having seen Jesus.

After serving nearly a lifetime as a chaplain, I love to share this message to others: Be open to the extraordinary. Don't get limited and distracted by all the earthly activities. Some say that earth is a school and there are only two classes we need to take. One course is how do I better love? The second course is how do I better serve? All the other learning activities we get caught up in are really extracurricular.

Each of us has opportunities in these temporary bodies of ours. We have the sacred presence of a soul. The soul is in communion with our Creator. Part of our charge is to try to find how to strengthen that connectivity. Know that the love of God is continually showering down. But not receiving it is a bit like having a house with electricity and not turning the lights on. We are all in charge of our own light switch. We can find ways to connect to God and enjoy when that happens.

FURTHER REFLECTION

This testimony underscores the profound reality of life beyond death and the significance of spiritual readiness. Witnessing a death vision reveals that our earthly existence is just a part of our journey. The presence of loved ones and Jesus welcoming someone home highlights the importance of nurturing our relationship with God and living a life of love and service.

Reflect on how you can better prepare for your eternal home. Consider the ways you can deepen your love for others and your service to God. Think about your daily actions and choices. Are they aligned with your spiritual goals? How can you strengthen your connection with God and live a life that reflects His love and grace?

PRAYER

Lord, thank You for the assurance of eternal life and the comforting presence You provide at the end of our earthly journey. Help us to live each day with a focus on loving and serving others. Guide us to strengthen our relationship with You and to keep our spiritual priorities in mind amidst life's distractions. May we find peace in knowing that You are always with us, ready to welcome us home. Amen.

CLOSING

WHAT DO WE TAKE FROM THESE TESTIMONIES?

I trust you are inspired, but I pray that you will also be moved at a heart level to know the One who was sacrificed for our sins, the miracle worker, the light of the world, the embodiment of perfect love, Jesus Christ.

People often ask what I have learned from years of recording testimonies. What do they reveal collectively? How have these revelations changed me? While I am not a prophet, nor a scholar, and still have so much to learn, there are a few things I know for sure.

MY VIEW OF GOD HAS CHANGED

He is MORE real, more present, more powerful, more loving, more merciful, more strategic, more gracious than I could have ever imagined. He absolutely has a plan for each of us. There will be times in life where we can't make sense of what is happening, and we will have to choose to trust Him. The timing of His plan is generally never what we desire or expect. I believe He can only reveal His plan in pieces because if we saw the whole plan, we likely would not understand it, and we would probably be too afraid to take the next step. When we become proud or succumb to our selfish desires, we block or hinder God's perfect plan. When we set our focus and hearts on Jesus, surrender to Him fully with gratitude and praise, walking in humility and obedience, we accelerate God's plan.

While God is so much more than what He can do for us, He continues to be a worker of miracles. He is still a supernatural God capable of healing, resurrecting the dead, and performing any other type of miracle we can or cannot fathom. He is worthy of our praise, worship, and reverence, whether we receive His miracles or not.

I continue to learn and grow as I seek Him. As I listen to these powerful testimonies and take them to the Word of God, many of the scriptures are clearly highlighted. It cannot be overstated: in these days where deception is rampant, it is imperative to take everything back to the scriptures and ask God to reveal His truth.

THE WAY I VIEW PEOPLE HAS CHANGED

I grew up as a conservative Christian. It was not uncommon to hear people in my community refer to people by their denomination. I never perceived it was in a derogatory way, but I think it led me to put people in boxes. Reflecting on when I felt the Lord tell me to "keep Him at the center" instead of focusing on their denomination, I feel He was asking me to break up the boxes where I place people. He wanted me to be free of the fear of man and trust His leading. Of course, the biggest box I had to shatter in this journey was the one that I placed around God.

I realize now that I don't keep those boxes as I did before this journey. It is no longer my Messianic Jewish friend, my Catholic friend, my Baptist friend, my Pentecostal friend, my Church of God friend. Now these people are just people that I care about, people that need Jesus. We are all broken people who need Jesus. As I connect with them, I can sense whether they are filled with the Holy Spirit. It doesn't seem to matter to me these days what sign is on the front of their church, but what is in their hearts. I do absolutely believe Jesus is the only way, as the Bible says (John 14:6), and that there is only one Bible (Revelation 22:18-19).

I think about heaven, and I imagine it this way: There will no longer be boxes and barriers. We will all be united in spirit with Jesus at the center. As it states in John 17:21: "I pray that they will all be one, just as you and I are one—as you are in me, Father, and I am in you. And may they be in us so that the world will believe you sent me" (NLT).

MY DEFINITION OF MINISTRY HAS CHANGED

I remember Heather's words so vividly: "We would love for you to come speak to our Bible study group about your ministry." My reply was immediate in correcting the obvious error: "I host a podcast. I don't run a ministry, but if you give me an idea of what you want me to share, I will consider speaking." If you asked for my definition of ministry at that time, I would have envisioned the loved and respected Billy Graham at his podium in a stadium being led by God, preaching to thousands of people. A noble and worthy, upright, faith-filled person, obedient in training with years of theology and wisdom brimming from their lips. I would have told you that these anointed people of God are given special gifts and assignments from God. I wouldn't have admitted this piece, but I also had the idea that these people live in a supernatural protective bubble where they don't face many trials because of their steadfast faith. I know it is comical now, but this is what I believed.

My "new and edited" definition of ministry is simply loving and/or serving the people you have contact with each day with the gifts or talents you have been given in a way that honors God and points people to Jesus. We have an opportunity every single day to be a vessel for God. We get to be part of that mosaic of His power and love that is lighting up around the globe that Billy Graham prophesied!

PRAYER IS ABSOLUTELY ESSENTIAL

One of the most important things to take from reading these powerful testimonies is the undeniable power of prayer. Our prayers are supernatural dynamite! We see this in every single testimony.

"True prayer is neither a mere mental exercise nor a vocal performance.
It is far deeper than that; it is a spiritual transaction
with the Creator of Heaven and Earth."

-Charles Spurgeon

Prayer is key in our relationship with God. It plays a role in miracles, yes, but it is also aligning our heart and mind with God. Is it not a miracle that we can speak to the Creator, our Savior, anytime and anyplace about anything? I believe if we really understood the power of prayer, we would stay on our knees and pray without ceasing.

Reading God's Word is the surest, easiest way to hear God speak to you. Taking time to be still and listen is also part of the process in hearing from Him. God is never going to tell you to do something that contradicts His Word.

FULL SINCERE SURRENDER CHANGES EVERYTHING

As I shared earlier, I was a Christian most of my life, yet I was terrified to fully surrender my life to Jesus. In retrospect, I see that God's plan was better for me than I could have imagined. God knows the gifts He has created in you. He knows the plan that is best. His plan for me was better than the one I had for myself. It doesn't mean it is always easy or comes without challenges, but all of it serves a purpose.

"The cave you fear to enter holds the treasure you seek."
-Joseph Campbell

The Holy Spirit is real, accessible, and will transform everything about your life. Your full surrender allows the Holy Spirit to move in a more powerful way. Many share that their understanding of the Bible increased dramatically after receiving the Holy Spirit. Typically, people see an increase in their spiritual senses and begin hearing from God in new and more powerful ways (promptings, dreams, visions, revelations).

I know it can feel scary, but trust God and His perfect plan for your life. Those that have taken the leap and fully surrendered can assure you that the benefits greatly outweigh the risks. The best part of the journey is growing closer to God and learning more about His heart along the way.

ONLY GOD

"Honey, that's you! He's talking about you!" my husband Lars announced. While surfing videos one evening, Glenn Beck appeared on the screen and shared a memory of his friend Billy Graham. It was a few years before his passing. They were discussing the sad and divided state of the world. "Billy, where are the people that are going to step up? Where's the next George Washington, the next Abe Lincoln, the next Billy Graham?" Glenn implored.

Billy smiled and answered: "God is tired of people like me getting credit for His work. It's not going to work that way this time. This time, people who are just regular people are going to do something that they may think is small and insignificant, and they may not even understand it, but they feel compelled that they're supposed to do this one thing. They'll argue in their own head and say, 'That doesn't make any sense. Why would I do that? That's not going to change anything.' And if everybody who hears what they're supposed to do and does just that—nothing more, nothing less, just that—and remains faithful, the lights will come on, and you'll see a mosaic that God is working, and everyone on Earth will know that only the God of Abraham, Isaac, and Jacob could have done it."

Glenn Beck continued sharing a story about one of these regular people. A 31-year-old man who was hopeless and at rock bottom surrendered his life to God. The turnaround in this man's life was miraculous. He wrote a song that went viral on the internet and soon found himself with open doors that could only be an act of God. The young man was invited to some of the biggest secular platforms in the world. He opened the Bible, sharing scripture, pieces of his testimony, and the God who had saved him. Glenn Beck sat in amazement, reflecting on the conversation he had with Billy Graham and seeing exactly what he had prophesied come to pass.

My husband continued: "Do you see it? You are one of the people he is talking about." We watched the clip again. I reflected back over the previous years. God brought to my memory so many of the moments I have shared with you in this book. The moment I heard His voice in the operating room that day: "This part of your life is over." The moment in the back of an ambulance when I prayed with desperation: "God, please let me share You with one more person…anyone."

Three years later, God would give me a vision to start a podcast. Even though it was so clear, it didn't make sense to me. I didn't think it would have an impact. I didn't feel I was qualified. I didn't even listen to podcasts! I had forgotten about my desperate ambulance prayer, but God remembered. Billy Graham's words kept resonating in my spirit: "And if everybody who hears what they're supposed to do and does just that—nothing more, nothing less, just that—and remains faithful, the lights will come on, and you'll see a mosaic that God is working, and everyone on Earth will know that only the God of Abraham, Isaac, and Jacob could have done it."

Suddenly, it started to become so clear to me. Yes, I am one of those regular people that God has used in a way I never knew was possible. In a way that only He could. And while He was working through me, He was working in me. I reflected on the guests and how each one is also part of that huge beautiful mosaic. Dean Braxton sharing his testimony about Jesus in schools, in groups that are lost in the occult, and many other places. William Harper sharing his miracle testimony in the jails and prisons. My mind reflected on each guest and how God is positioning them in specific places all around the world, in front of different people and groups that are far from God. "God is strategic, working behind the scenes in ways we cannot understand," as expressed by several of the guests.

I reflected on the Spark Media Podcast conference where I met so many beautiful souls who have also been called to step out and use their voices to share the love of Christ. God is moving the church outside of its walls and into the streets, into places where the love of Jesus is desperately needed through regular people that are compelled by His call! The mosaic began appearing in my mind. I could see the globe covered in darkness, with His light and love appearing, breaking through, joining together, and spreading out, defeating the darkness!

I sat in tears of complete awe. God answered my prayer in a way I could have never imagined. Instead of allowing me to share Him with one more person, He allowed me to share Him with millions of people and in countries around the globe. What a blessing to see His hand at work through a wider lens!

"Now to Him who is able to do immeasurably more than all we ask or imagine, according to His power that is at work within us, to Him be glory in the church and in Christ Jesus throughout all generations, forever and ever! Amen."
- Ephesians 3:20-21

INVITATION: IN CHRIST WE ARE A NEW CREATION!

My prayer for you as this book comes to a close is that you are not left simply inspired, but you have a new understanding that God is for you too, that He loves you, and that your life can look so different walking with Him. I hope you also see that He can work miracles through you too!

Have you accepted Jesus Christ as your Savior? The good news is that you can do this anywhere, and all you need is a sincere and open heart to seek Him.

"You will find me when you seek me with all of your heart."
- Jeremiah 29:13

If you are ready to ask Jesus into your life:

Heavenly Father,

I come to You in the name of your precious Son, Jesus. I want to know You. Thank You for sending your one and only Son to die on a cross and forgive my sins. Come into my life. I repent of my sins. Make me new. Help me to walk in the plans that You have for me. Help me to become the person that You created me to be and to live a life that brings You glory. I ask this in the name of Jesus.

Congratulations if you said that prayer! You just made the most important decision of your life! Heaven is rejoicing over you (Luke 15:7)!

MY PRAYER FOR YOUR NEXT STEPS

Accepting Jesus is a huge step! Congratulations! It is the first step in a beautiful relationship with your Savior, and here are some things I would offer as you grow in your faith and your knowledge of Him and all that He has for and through you:

1. Start a daily practice of prayer, surrender, and scripture. Even if you start with five minutes each morning with a devotional that gives you one verse, start and notice the impact. Be expectant for more peace, more promptings, more clarity, more joy, more JESUS!

2. Ask God to lead you to a small group. Repeatedly, when I ask people of strong faith about their faith walk, it is common to hear how joining the right small group, whether prayer or Bible study, was life-changing and elevated their faith to a new level. My prayer is that you find a group with a humble and loving leader who is continually growing in knowledge of scripture. It may take time to find the right group, but keep praying and ask God to give you discernment and wisdom.

3. Ask God to provide a mentor. As you navigate your new group or Bible study, you will meet many types of people. God has sent people into my life when I have prayed for a wise mentor. They have blessed me in the most amazing ways. Sometimes they come for a season and help me with a specific issue. Sometimes God sends them to be a listening and loving ear as I am processing hard things I don't understand or may not want to share in a group. While I have not always had a mentor, I have had this prayer answered several times, and it has been invaluable.

4. Accept God's grace and mercy in this ongoing process of sanctification. Yes, He has given us free will, and we have choices to make every day. There are no perfect people outside of Jesus. We all have things to learn, and we can be a vessel of service, His mouthpiece. We have free will. We can be obedient with the things He is offering, or we can refuse. Know that His presence and His love for us is unchanging. Our salvation is not earned but is through grace by faith in Jesus Christ. All of us fall short, but in Him, we are a new creation. Through repentance and faith in Jesus, we have the promise of salvation.

5. If God is clearly compelling you to step out in faith into a specific

calling, I encourage you to do it. Please understand that God can use anyone. Remember the scripture that His power works best in weakness. Trust Him and pray into whatever you feel He is putting on your heart. I think about all the things I would have missed out on if I had chickened out. The wonderful people I have connected with, the miracles I have heard, and learning more about who God really is! I encourage you today, when He compels you…have the faith to take the first step and trust it.

THE CHOICE IS YOURS TODAY

We can invite Jesus into our lives. We can choose to surrender to His will, invite Him in to search us, equip us, forgive us, convict us, empower us, fill us with His love, peace, and joy. Each day we can choose to say yes to Him and be His light on the Earth. We can be a part of the beautiful mosaic He is orchestrating around the globe!

MY PRAYER FOR YOU

Dear Heavenly Father,

Thank you for the precious soul reading this book. Thank you for the testimonies contained in this book and for the testimonies contained in Your Holy Word. Thank you that Your strength works perfectly in weakness! Thank you for allowing me to be a vessel. I pray on behalf of this beautiful soul that you would lead them by faith and not by sight. I pray you would give them a new hunger and understanding of Your Word. I pray you would help them to see You for who You really are. I ask you to help them to forgive others who have wounded them, to bring healing to their hurts. Draw their hearts to Yours. We thank You that Your Word says anyone who believes in Jesus will not perish but will have eternal life (John 3:16). We thank You that You created this person with a plan and a purpose with unique gifts. I ask You to open their spiritual senses that they would hear, see, feel, and know Your voice in new ways. As You lead them each day, fill them with boldness. I pray You would multiply what is in their hands for the work of their calling and that it brings You glory. I thank You for the breakthroughs You are sparking! In Jesus' name!

"I pray that out of His glorious riches He may strengthen you with power through His Spirit in your inner being so that Christ may dwell in your hearts through faith. And I pray that you, being rooted and established in love, may have power, together with all the Lord's holy people, to grasp how wide and long and high and deep is the love of Christ, and to know this love that surpasses knowledge—that you may be filled to the measure of all the fullness of God. Now to Him who is able to do immeasurably more than all we ask or imagine, according to His power that is at work within us, to Him be glory in the church and in Christ Jesus throughout all generations, forever and ever! Amen."

- Ephesians 3:16-21

ABOUT THE AUTHOR

Julie is a lover of Jesus Christ, a wife, mom, and the creator and host of the *Everyday Miracles* Podcast. Her show was awarded "Most Bingeworthy Podcast" at the 2023 Christian Spark Media conference. Julie is passionate about sharing powerful testimonies that glorify God and inspire hope and faith. She has witnessed some miraculous things in her personal life and in her nursing career of over 20 years, and loves to share that Jesus is very real and still performing wonders.

Professionally, Julie loved serving as a nurse. She worked for two years in a cardiovascular intensive care unit, then pursued a Master of Science degree and enjoyed a 16-year career as a certified registered nurse anesthetist. In 2009, she was recognized by the Mecklenburg Times as a Healthcare Hero. She is presently enjoying being a wife and mom, making new friends through her show, and sharing their amazing faith experiences.

Everyday Miracles Podcast is available on YouTube, Spotify, Apple Podcasts, Stitcher, iHeartRadio, and has covered the globe with millions of downloads. Follow *Everyday Miracles Podcast* on Instagram and Facebook for new episodes and updates!

To contact Julie, or review the growing list of testimonies: http://everydaymiraclespodcast.com/